Hearts On A Page

Independently Published
with Draft2Digital eBook,
a division of Draft2Digital

draft2digital.com

First Edition
10 9 8 7 6 5 4 3 2 1

ISBN: 9798201227173

Editor: Laika, Jessica, Theyonna, Caren
Cover Design by Laika Constantino
Cover Made with Canva
Author Photo by Gavin Mendoza

Hearts On A Page
Volume 3

Laika Constantino

To all the women who came before me,
You loved yourself better than I could.

Introduction

I remember being told that I wasn't good enough to do something I've always wanted to do. We are all guilty of telling ourselves we are not good enough to enjoy the little things that make us who we are. We are a shiny new car that he just forgot to drive around the neighborhood.

As I've said in the previous volume, Twenty-first Century love is different. It makes us rethink the things that hurt us as we grow old. We grow old and there's nothing we can do about it. In a Century, the love that we know will be revoked into a tale told by our great grandchildren. But who knows what the Twenty-second century will be all about? We'll be gone by then.

I remember listening to the stories of my grandparents and how they fell in love. That was the Twentieth Century. I once thought that it was something special but I've met so many boys who would change my mind about love. Love is incandescent. Love is a longing to be something you want to be. As I write this to Lana Del Rey's *Lust For Love*, I know that things change like the seasons.

Love isn't what Carole Landis once knew. She died because of who she loved. I wish she knew that she has a world of people who wanted her to love and love and love. She deserved at least a second chance in love. I wrote from her perspective throughout this series. She is the reason why I can write about the depression that I once had. Just like from drugs, you can relapse from depression. I should know. I've been there before.

A wise poet once said, "a future was once lost yesterday." She said it on April 18. Sylvia Plath knew what she was writing. She wrote about how she felt. She loved poetry and the people she knew. She felt so many feelings that made her wonder. She wrote it all down. And like Carole Landis, she ended her life. Why? That's the question that burns my mind.

Self-love is more important than any other love. You must have faith in yourself because the world needs more people writing about how they feel. Love what makes you who you are. Always.

With all my heart,
Laika
xo

I Knew You All Along

I knew you
and how you'd change
the ending,
and how everything
that I believed in
means nothing
to you.

I knew you...
I knew you.

I know you favorite songs
I knew you all along
so why am I the one
to see you with her?

I hope you know
that the pain
you've caused
is never-ending.
It's never-ending.

Trouble

In sunsets and sunrise,
I want to spend with you
I could fall for something
that's worthwhile.

I hope that it's not
any trouble that
I wrote your name
for all to see,
for all to know.

But why you chose to hide
when the spotlight's all
that you've got to keep
your company.

I hope that you remember
all the trouble
that we've both caused
for each other.

(Was it ever enough?
I guess not.)

The Last Time

It was the last time we got together.
And when you kissed me,
I never knew it'll be our last.
But darling, I wished it wasn't.

I wished it wasn't
the last time that we spoke,
that we got together.

I wished that we had more time
to spend together
than the one that we got.

The Show

Darling, when summer ends
I wanted to get
those memories back.
You said sorry
a million times
but I knew
it was for show.

Darling,
I'd rather feel this
emptiness inside of me.
I'd rather feel
like there's nothing wrong
with how our story ended.
But something was,
something was wrong
with the way our story ended
and that broke my heart in two.

Young Girl

Young girl
ridden with scandal.
A gentleman
spending all his time
on a girl like her.

But why does
she seem okay
when she wonders
about him
at night.

"Is she okay?"
"Is she doing fine?"
You may ask someone
she knows
so dearly.

But at sixteen,
she was just a young girl
who wanted to see the stars.
Her heart seems to love it.

His Eyes So Blue

His eyes so blue
I drown and drown
over and over again.

But will he save me?
I sure hope so.

And then love drives me crazy.
It fades into darkness
once I get more crazy.

Will I ever stay the same?
I sure hope so.

I say, "darling,
there's always something
that ruined us but it never
ruined me."

I hope
he knew that.

I hope he knew how to mend
a person through her heart.

Complicated

Darling,
There's nothing
more in life
than what complicates it.

And what complicates it
is the way you saw
the worst in me.

You wanted to see me down
when all that I wanted was the world.

You wanted nothing
but to love the world
and to be loved in return.
I just wanted you.

Hoax

You are someone who I've spent
my days with if I've ever written
a melody all by myself.

You are someone who knows
that I know nothing of
the pain that others bestow upon me.

You are someone who I could
love once more if
things were different.

Darling, it's so frustrating.
Darling, it's so much of a hoax
and I believe it because you are it.

You are someone
that I dearly love.

For You

For you,
I would wish
on a thousand
stars in the sky.

For you,
I'd risk it everything
that I fell in
love with.

For you,
I watch the clouds
pass us by.

For you,
I'm brand new...

(But my heart can never be
mended the same way.)

Chase

You chased me
only to forget
why you loved me.

You chased me
only to fall
for something
I never wanted
to be a part of.

You chased me
only to make me cry inside.

Darling, I never cried so hard
at the ending
I never saw it coming.

It Did

We had something
that would last
for what it's worth.

I'd love you again
and again
until I pull the breaks
on us.

I've never
wanted it to end
this way.

But it did.
Darling, it did.

Film

I seen so many films
about a love so pure
but the ending
always haunted me.

I wished it never
ended that way.

I wished it never
had the ending
that it did
because I loved,
and loved
how the tale
progressed.

My heart could handle that.
I know it can.

Voices

Darling, I heard from
the voices that surrounded
me. I knew nothing much
that's what they say
but I knew what's best
for me and that's not you.

The last thing that they said to me
was sorry for causing you pain.

(The pain that I never saw coming.)

Muse

You paint the flowers
just to paint the trees.

You saw the colors
that reigned brighter
than the sun.

You seek the words
that's left unspoken
and deliver the things
that words tend to leave.

You are that to me, my love.
You are someone that made me care
about the things
that never mattered to anyone else
but in our world...
It did.

Truth

The truth is its better
if you don't explain
how you lost me but honey,
you did lose me
for whatever reason
that we both don't know.

The truth is its better
if you didn't come around.
I'm doing better in a world
without the cruelty
that you've done to my heart.

I've Been

I've been shamed
for writing about
what's going on.

I've been on the side
of fearing what
could have been
rather than
what's meant to be.

I've been called
manipulative
and worse,
stupid and crazy.

I've been called things
that broke me in two.

You can't tell me
that anymore.

(My heart has grown
without you.)

Twisted

You twisted the truth
because you wanted
a win in chaotic times.

You made sure
that I'd lose in a fight
that you've already won.

You are that twisted
and that is cruel.
You knew that I loved you
like I loved LA.
You knew that my heart
can't handle the breaks
that you caused.

Defend

You've defended
your homeland
but you never did
defended me.

I could've been your Queen
and you, my King
but we are lost
in this world.

Darling, I don't want
to stand around pretending
everything is alright.
I want to rule the world.

I want to rule the world
and be the Queen of hearts.

Dream

Don't tell me
not to dream
when all my
dreams came true.

But darling,
the fates doesn't
own your dreams.

You do.

You own the dreams
that you dream
and the words that you
dare to speak.
You dared to speak.

Who am I to tell you
that the world
deserves better hearts
colliding into one?
Who am I to tell you that?

Ruins

Don't ruin my good name.
I've been an angel
all my life, darling.

Don't call me a rebel
as I haven't rebelled
since I was twelve.

Don't tell me to think straight.
I've been thinking straight since
it was the best thing
that I've done for myself.

Just don't do that to me again.
You know how much I can't handle
another broken heart.

True

I've spent my days thinking if it's true
that the day you'd say hello was the day
you'd find me riding around with the old strings
that pulls us together like the stars brightening
up the night sky.

Oh, how I wonder about the day
we'd rule the world.
Just tell me so and I'll ride
the waves with you.

Darling, I'd ride
the waves with you.

(Darling, it's true...)

Wild

Where do the wild things go?
When everything falls apart
When everything ends
like how the ocean
calls for a new tomorrow.
I hope to live to see
that call to the wild.

Where does the wild things go
when everything around us
has all died out?
Oh, where?
Where does it all go?

Oh, tell me where?
Where does it all go
when things aren't
as it seems?

Tell me where do broken hearts go
when there's nothing,
nothing left for them to love?

I've Tried

I've seen the existence of the unimaginable.
I've flooded the roads with the rain.
I've tried to rescue those you set aside.
And you've set aside so many who never
knew you.

How I've tried to be the hero
of the story but all that you see
is a damsel in distress.

At least, I've tried.
I've tried.

Helpless

I was a curious child.
I'm always asking questions
to those around me.
But I was tongue tied,
I had no other choice.
I had to keep on asking.
I had to keep on going.
But I was young,
what do I know about things?
I'm helpless.
I'm helpless.

I Love

You said that I was making you
uncomfortable but darling,
that's how I love.

I love like there's no end to this Earth.
I love like the days past.

Oh, how the days pass by me
like starlight shining brightly
across the sky.

Darling, I love like there's no ends
to this Earth because there truly isn't one.

Sapphire

You said that
those who were made of stars
shimmer like sapphires
and the galaxies and the universe
aligns whenever you see me smile.

I said,
"you're bluffing."
But honey,
you argued and said,
"it's true."

Stop

Stop worrying about those
who aren't around anymore.
They're not in you life for a reason
and that reason is crucial
to your well being.

Stop pretending that everything is okay.
Speak up and say what's really going on
Because honey, we're all human.
We all strive for a better tomorrow.
We all want the same things
And that's to be free.

Love Is Simple

Someone once said that love is simple
and I think it's so but make sure
that the person you love
leaves you breathless because it's the little
things that count when it comes to love.

A Movie Without You

I was a movie without you
but it reminded me of how we used to be
and how I didn't like the ending.

You said that I was crazy to watch
it without you but without you
I learned how to love who I am.

Closure

I spent days finding closure
But you took my fragile heart
And tore it into two pieces
like a broken heart wanting to mend.
I never cried so much
before I knew that it was all for show.
Darling, I'm not like the others
and you knew that I needed you
even if it's only for show.

I need to remember you
that way even if it's just for show.
So... goodbye, my love.
Goodbye for now.

Wound

You spent your days
wondering if he'd notice
all the things
that you'd do
if you were his.

And then,
love was the one thing
you'd give to him
but he gave you nothing
in return.

(Honey,
don't love him
and the wound will heal
in return.)

Hidden Love

I took a napkin
and wrote something down
to write to you
but I never wanted for you
to see it.

I wanted to hide
every heartache,
every little piece of me
from you
but you wanted me
and my love.
I don't know why
but you seemed
to care about me.

I don't know why
you loved me
like you did
but you did.
And for that I am
forever grateful.

Though I Loved You

Though I loved you
I'm alright, my dear,
on my own loving who I am.
I wished that it didn't end
that way.
I wish that it still were us.
Darling, I loved you.
No. I still love you.

What I Wanted

I wanted to start over.
I wanted to love you
like the first time round.
I wanted nothing to do
with the spotlight
but you brought me
into a world
that I did not want anything
to do with.
But you,
you wanted so much
just to keep me
from hurting.
I wanted to start over.
I didn't get that from you
so this must be a goodbye.

(Goodbye, my love.)

Neile Adams

I was a convent girl
with a reputation to uphold.
You were a rebel
with a heart of gold.

I said,
"I've never been
riding before."
But you made me
feel safe and secure
that was the first date.

I took my time
to love you
but was it enough?

I told them
that you could be
a pain when your bad
and adorable
when you're good.

And you know,
it's damn true.

Carole Lombard

I was the funny girl.
You were the man
everyone wanted.
I was the girl
you chased.

And boy,
the victor can stake his claim
But it wasn't that easy
to love a man like you.
But I was in love…
And it wasn't for show.

Word on the street
that you had her
name on your lips,
But if I come to you,
would you kiss me
like you used to?
Would you love me
like you did before?

Darling,
when I said
my vows
I meant it
and I'll keep it
till my dying day.

I was scared

for what lies ahead,
for the things
that escaped my lips.
But it didn't stop me,
from being the woman
you needed.

Darling, I will come home
to you again.
I promise.
I promise, I will
even if it kills me.

Debbie Reynolds

You used to write me
into the melody and said,
"Darling, you're my muse."

I guess, it did not occur to me
that things ended
the way that it did.

I'm certain that you'd come around
but I wished that I'd listen
to all the warning signs
that Frank had laid out for me.

I didn't
because I love you so much
that it pains me
to see you happy
with her,
with Elizabeth.

I remember that you used to write me
into a melody that said,
"Darling, you're my forever"
and I believed it.

Expired

Darling, I wanted so much
than to love you until our dying day
but you wanted to keep
something in your mind
that I wanted to erase.
I knew you'd only sing
if she was still around.

(Our love expired
the day you said
goodbye forever.)

My Heart Believed

My fragile state can't handle
the things you made her believe in.
You made her believe in
everything and in nothing.
And I wished for things to be different,
I wish that they didn't see you
as the man who lost his way.
They didn't see what I saw in you
when they said that you'll only hurt me.
My delicate heart believed in you
so much that only little the little things pass her by
like little birds flying above her head.
No, they didn't see what I saw.

But I could imagine what may be
and what is used to be
by leaving and caring
for something that
isn't written down for her
to say out loud.
She could stop pretending once
the damage is done
but there'll be so much damage
for one person to get lost in.
And all that they could say to her
was you aren't thinking straight.
I was. I was thinking straight.

All that they could say
when you love someone,

you start thinking of them
with the lights out.
They said once you are in love,
you start feeling like the world
is empty without them.
But they didn't tell you,
the things that he'll say to you
once he finds himself
in someone else's arms
that's not your own.

My dear heart, will you still believe him?
Will you follow him into the spotlight?
I think I will if he'd let me.
I think I will if he'd let me.

Main Street

I take the winding road
as I walk down Main Street.
I don't even know how to
and when to catch my breath
as I gaze out at the open sea.
I saw you and I knew you.
I wish I was at the lakes
where you first saw me.
I wish I wasn't walking down
this long road without you.
I wish I was with you
dancing around
the living room floor,
but I'm alone
wishing that one day
you'll walk down
Main Street with me.

I Really Wish You'd Say It To My Face

I really wish you'd say it to my face.
I really wish you'd tell me you love me
without thinking about what's next.
I really wish you'd come back to me
instead of leaving and flying to New York.
You left me out here in the West
where it's cold and dreary
without someone who could love like I do.
How could you do that to me?
How could you go away like that without
telling me goodbye?

Black Cadillac

We're driving around in your black Cadillac
speaking as if we knew each other
from way back when but we don't know.
We don't know when things
will go back to normal again
so that we can drive away together,
the two of us driving far away
just like how it used to be.

Stay

There's no way that you've forgotten
about me when your eyes remembers
all the pain that we've both gone through.
But you thought that I'd leave so easily
because of the things you've said to me,
I didn't. I stayed knowing you'll find
your way back to me. It kills me to know
you're not around to tell me you love me.
I wish you stayed instead of leaving.
So, please, stay and don't leave me alone.

James Dean

Darling, you've caught yourself in the middle
of a war in which you never wanted to be in.

You wanted no part of it.
You wanted to be the master of your own tracks.
You wanted someone to match your potential
but I'm not her.
I'm not the one who will be Natalie Wood
on the silver screen.

I've never matched your speed.
Darling, you're James Dean
the highway will catch up to you.
The saddest thing is that
I think it already did
But I'm not afraid to let you go
Because you played me like a fiddle.

Darling, you've caught yourself in the middle
of a war in which you never wanted to be in.

I get that you wanted to fight your own battles
but honey, I know that it's a lost cause
when we rebel against something that
we have no choice but to sink ourselves into.

Bare

You saw me bare.
I saw you lick your lips
like a tiger hunting
for his next meal.
You made me chuckle
but that didn't change
how you left me alone,
that didn't change
how you didn't hear
my beating heart stop
for a moment.
You saw me bare
and I didn't mind.

I Finally Love Him

He hitched up a plan
to make me fall for him.
And I finally love him.
I finally love him.
So, please, tell him
I'll be around
once again.
Just make him promise
to wait for me.

True Love

True love doesn't make
the world goes round.
It stops for just one moment
before it continues to revolve
around the sun again.

Lost Girl

You lost me
like Peter lost Wendy.
Darling, you knew,
I grew up
and you stayed
the same playing
every childish game
in the book of
never ever growing up.

You lost me
like I was the lost girl
who took matters
into her own hands
and rescued the boys
that needed rescuing.

Darling,
You'll lose me.

You lost the love
that I gave to you
when you chose her
over me.

I Want You

I want you to love me
because I've never felt
like this for someone before.
I want you to fuck me
because you touching me
is something that's been
in my mind for the past
few weeks, few months.
I just want you and only you.

Here We Go Again

Here we go again
fighting about nothing
just because one of us
said to the other
that things aren't the same.
Here we go again
chasing each other
around the house
trying to make a point.
But here we go again,
not making any sense to the other
because that's what people
think about us, right?
Not making any sense.
Not figuring about how we feel.
So, here we stand in a quiet room
waiting for the other to utter a word.

After A Fight

There's clothes on the floor
from last night's rendezvous.
My handbag and its contents
scattered on the floor
by the bedside table
because I got mad at you
and tossed my lipstick
towards you with such ease.
But I didn't know what to expect
when you began to kiss me,
the love making started
and I became yours again.

I Love For Us

I love for us to stay the same
but if we do, would how we love
each other changes?
I don't know what it is
when it comes to us.
I'd take each armor
and lay them down
to end whatever we fought about,
but I just wish that you made me
yours a lot quicker than
I'd hope you would.
My love, we are like the Earth
as it rotates around the sun.
We spun in circles, twice through.
So, I left my high heels
on the foot of the bed
as we're intertwined
under these sheets.

Not That Kind Of Girl

I let you pocket my undergarment
just to let you know that I'd stay.
But if you are looking for a one night stand,
I'm not that kind of girl.
So, I kept an open mind
when it comes to you
and what I've written about us.
But understand this,
I'm not the kind of girl
who would get up and leave.
I'd stay.
I'd stay.

Undress Me

I can see it in your eyes
the way that you look at me.
It makes me wonder
how much and how long
you're willing to wait
for someone like me
to arrive within your reach.
But I'm right here,
wanting for you
to undress me.
I want you to see me
vulnerable and bare.
Because I know how long
your days are and
how tired you must be.
So, in the end of the day,
I'm always here for you.
I'm always the girl
waiting for you
to come home to her.

Skin

I feel your skin on my skin
and every little thing
that makes you brilliant as a lover.
You are the one thing
and you are so much
of what people call too good.
You can be a pain at times
but that doesn't mean
I don't love you.
I love all of you
and letting our skins touch
is something that I can do
without having to tell you
that I'm in love with you.

Never One To Brag

I'm never one to brag
but my man is great.
He makes me feel
like I'm the best thing
that ever happened to him.
And when he undresses me,
he sees someone I never saw.
I'm never one to brag
but he's as charming
as what the other girls
are saying about him.
Given that I don't say it aloud,
but he knows what I've got
and what I've been hiding
from the rest of the world.
He's got that one thing
I've always looked for in a guy.
I'm never one to brag
but I love all of him
and he loves all of me.

In The Pouring Rain

I'm standing in the pouring rain
I had my best dress on
But I had no one to tell me
that I'm beautiful
but I'm standing there
waiting for you, babe.

Waiting for you
in the pouring rain...
So, we can dance until three
in the great outdoors
as it comes pouring down on us.

I've Had The Feeling

I've had the feeling
of regret when it comes
to betraying someone like you.
I've felt so much pain
in my heart when you left me.
I wanted for you to stay
and lay right next to me.
But I've never wanted
for us to fight until 2AM,
I just wanted you to love me
the way that I love you.

Music Captivates

Music captivates like those blue eyes of yours.
It's pure but how am I supposed to know
what comes after the rain when it comes to you.
Don't leave me stranded like you've done before.
Let's find a way to make the most of the night
and I'll make sure people will say we're sugar
when it comes to a love like ours.
Where do I begin when you're gone?
Do I start where the music entangles us?
Or how the music captivates our minds
when we leave the ground flying.
But I know, how music captivates
those who sees things differently
than the rest of the world.

The Profane Poet

I've got jokes people heard
and it's about us, my dear.
I'm not as profane as people think.
I'm not making things into a bigger
situation that it already is.
But whenever, I hear our song.
I hear a different beat
that aged like a fine wine.
I've got so much more
that I'll say to you
because people know I'm profane.
And I know you like me that way.

The Heart Knows

The heart knows what the mind doesn't.
I don't know where to begin
when it comes to ideas forming in my mind.
The heart knows what to do
when it comes down to independence.
I know that you can't figure out
what I have in store for myself.
But the heart knows it all too well.
So, let's take things slow
as I put on some Jazz music on the jukebox.
Let's take things slow
and mess around like the heart knows
what it is we're going to do
in the next hour or so.

This Was Your Doing

This was your doing.
You left me broken
on the front porch step.
This was your doing.
You left me crying
wondering what happened.
You left me thinking
what it is I've done
to lose you.
But I was told,
that it was your doing
by our friend and your ex.

The Feeling Of Lust

The feeling we solely take
for granted is something
that we rather keep to ourselves.
The feeling of love and the romance
that we've made in the past.
I knew that there was something
coming in the dark
as things are felt on the floor.
But I knew that it was the feeling
of love and lust and romance.
That's what we've got
and I think I like it.

My Only Obsession

There's one thing
I currently hold
so close to my heart.
He's like an illegal drug
when I was fresh
of the plane from Manila
to get addicted to.
And I'll know, if he's got a plane
to make me his in the morning.
He'll know, he'll be my only obsession
that I'll keep wanting to have
in the middle of the night.
He's charming full of wit
and those blue eyes of his
will be a gateway to a sweet addiction
I don't want to get
rehabilitated from.

The Taste Of Him

I can still taste his kiss on my lips.
It left such a surprising mark
on my rose colored lips.
I can still hear his voice
calling out my name
but not that it matters
when your stuck getting dressed
in front of the mirror.
But you can only see the things
that you wanted to see.
I can taste him in my mouth
as I trace my lips with my finger.
Not that it matters now
that he's around to watch me
slowly get dressed.

I'll Never Get Over You

I'll never get over you.
You were someone
who cared so much about me
that I've never thought
about anyone else.
I'll never get over how you
spoke so highly about us
to your friends back home.
I could never forget
how you made me believe
in fairytales again.
So, let me be the first to say,
"I'll never get over you
until my dying day."

He Never Knew

He never noticed
how my deep brown eyes
glistened in the dark.
He never wondered
what could've been
if it were him and I.
He never wanted
a girl from a far of place
that only came alive
in the night.
He never knew
how I changed
for him and his world.
But I noticed,
how his brown eyes
lit the night sky.
I wondered the things
that might have been
if it were him and I.
All that I ever could
want was in him
but he never noticed.

I Left The Door Open

I left the door open
just so he could watch me
get changed into something
more comfortable than a dress.
It wasn't that long ago
that his blue eyes
caught my every move.
He wore a navy blue t-shirt
as he stood by the doorway.
He didn't waste a single moment
with the time he's got.

The Feeling Of Lust, Pt. 2

I've turned every corner
driving in the driver's seat
like I've been drunk
on gin and tonic.
I haven't been drunk before
but it's besides the point.
I feel like I have to get undressed
just for you to see me again.
Just so you know, my darling,
we haven't seen each other
since last December.
And the feeling of lust
captivates my heart,
it's been driving everything
that you are to me.
But I'm not a bitch,
I'm not someone who clings
onto someone way too much.
I just feel lust and love
like it's all brand new to me.

I Should Be The Girl You're Sleeping With

I should be the girl you're sleeping with
but tonight is a different story.
You're with her in New York
and I'm in Portland
wondering if you're ever
going to see her again.

You've got her by your side
and you're in her bed.
I didn't think much of it.
I thought it was just a small fling
that will end before Valentine's Day
but it didn't. I didn't hear the end of it.

It's been a little long
that's what I'll do to pass the time.
I've been crying into my pillow
wondering who could heal
my broken heart and make me feel
like a new woman again.

His Girl

His girl has no filter.
She speaks like the boys
in the locker room.
His girl knows how to party
but all that he ever takes her to
is posh places that she feels
so different in.
His girl is unlike any other
girls that he's been with.
She's not too simple
but she keep her head
up in the clouds
when it comes to love.
"It's hopeless," they tell him,
"It's hopeless to fall
for a girl like that.
Stick to someone
who's more cultured than she."

I wish they knew what
it's like to be me,
to be someone with a heart so pure.
I wish they knew of the things
we do when no one is around.
I wish they knew what hopelessness
is truly defined by the bigots
and his harem full of women
going crazier for his time
than I could ever go.
But he and I both know,

his time is split between
his work and his girl.

And I'll let the world know, I'm his girl.

The Explorer

I want him to explore my body
like an explorer venturing to a land
no one has ever been to before.
I know the places he's been to
and I know all the street his walked on
but I haven't been to the place
where Romeo took Juliet
on their night out of town.

I want him to explore me
like I'm the road not taken.
I want him to taste me
like a kid in a candy store.
I know the little things
that made him curious
about how my body moves in the dark.

He played his ace.
I have him in my dock
ready to occupy my mind.

Touch

I don't see the harm
of a little rendezvous in the sheets,
a little flirting with my man
because every time he touch me
I melt a little inside.
I hate it when he's not around
and he knows it
and he know how to drive me crazy
when it comes to touching me in places
that I've never been touched before.
I don't see anything wrong
with how the world comes down at night.

Ask Me In Bed

If you want to know how to get
through to someone like me,
I'd write a poem for all the things
that made me fall in love with you.
You ask yourself if I'll read it
over and over again until I manage
to respond in prose and song.
Darling, if you want me,
I would ask me in bed to marry you.
But you know me so well,
you know I'd like to be asked
by a fountain that mirrors the soul.

British Boys

I thought I'd tell you
I've never gotten over
my love for British boys.
They're always on my mind
ever since I step foot on
American soil at thirteen.
There's never been a single
guy that I've come across
who could match their wit.
That's the thing that I love
about British boys
as well as their charms.
It never changes like how
many boys I've been with.

To tell you the truth,
you've always been on my mind
ever since we first met
and I hope you knew
what it's like not to be with you.
You are the one exception I've made.
You are that one person
I'll recognize it in my heart.
You've turned something in me
that made me want all that you are.
That's the thing I love about you.

British boys are different.
They aren't as wicked as American boys.
That much I know.

Let The Children Be Our Legacy

Let the children be our legacy
that we leave when we're gone.
Let the stars determine
what we can be in the future.
Let the world escape into the galaxy
of another piece of us
that lets us put our guard down.

What I know about the younger generation
is that they are smarter than we think?
They've got things figured out
we just bring them down
because that's what society is telling us.

So, let the children be our legacy
as they make the world so brand new.

Draw The Stars

You drew a picture in the sky
as the stars aligned like never before.
I saw my muse in a different light
as I spent the days thinking
about what you are about to do.
You've never took your eyes
away from my eye line.
I can't imagine a world
where we are far apart.

You've seen so many people
who loves what you do and loves you,
but I fear you'll end up with one of them,
I fear our love is only good in lust.
We hardly spoke of the stars that changed us.
But I don't fear the stars and the sky,
it draws like an arrow to my heart.
Though the picture is beautiful,
I only see the stars in the sky.

So, if you manage to draw with the stars,
Just know that I'm wondering if you're the one.

I'm Made Of Glass

I'm made of glass.
I can get broken
in many different ways.
People can see through me
when I try to speak a single word.

I don't know if it what I said
or it's the moments
we spent the night together.
People don't know the things
we talked about in bed.

I'm made of glass
but my heart is whole.
It used to be broken
from everything I used to hate.
We can handle anything
if it wasn't for the things we love.

I don't know what to make of it.
It's been making me run in circles
over and over again.
I couldn't tell if its me and you
or them trying to break us apart.

I should know how to write
when it comes to you
but I seem to write nothing
on the blank page.

I'm made of glass
but I don't know
how to make of it.
I don't know how I should act
when it comes to you.

You seem to leave an indentation
in my mind that I don't want to get rid of.

Can We Dance The Night Away?

Can we dance the night away
like Scott and Zelda did?
My teens had something
my twenties didn't.

It had the beauty of the waltz.
It had the glamor of Hollywood.
It had so much more than
what purple haze had.

It was in my teens that I died
in the inside with the fear of losing.
But I never knew that I lost myself
in the process of what the arts had.

Can we dance the night away?
Can we be intertwined as the music
gets us lost to the beat?
Can we be one once more?

I can still smell the odor it left.
I can still taste the alcohol
that we've drank together.
But we both knew it was wrong.

We did it anyway.
We did the things that people
can't stay away from.
But how can they know?

We're only human after all.
We're only seeing the things
that made us dance
like they did in the Twenties.

These Ivory Walls

These ivory walls
I've painted on
over moments and time.
And I don't regret it.
It's been a dream of mine
to leave my mark
and leave something
that people can talk about
when all my days are through.

These ivory walls will be the piece
I leave for those to remember me by.
People will know the love that I had
with one man who saw what I didn't
see in myself for a time.

And on these walls are the stories,
that will be passed down
from generations to come.

Because I knew all the things
my man did when I wasn't around.
He's my muse and I'm in his pretty head
just waiting for something to come along.

But if I waited for things,
I wouldn't be able to learn
and grow into who I want to be.
It's not a crime to be loved
by someone who wanted

a woman who knows what
she is to a world that just wants
to break her apart.

These ivory walls
I've painted on
can only show the memories
people talked about.

But what I've written down,
are the memories that made
me love him even if time
wasn't on our side
for so much of the story.

And he said, "we've made
most of the story turn into folklore"
when they saw us around
in love or fighting about the things
that happened in the past.

He said, "darling, what's wrong?"
when all that I could do was cry.

But we are still in the beginning of it all,
I'm just a romantic reminiscing about
the things that could happen
if we quarantined in Atlanta, Georgia
away from the stresses of all the hell
the world would drive into the picture.

But I just hear a Lana Del Rey song

in my quiet room at my mother's house,
it said, "I just want to dance with you"
and that's what I'll do after reading
Sylvia Plath and Emily Dickinson
to keep you in my heart and my mind.

Like Zelda, I'll save you the waltz
when you come by to stop me from crying.

Between these ivory walls are the stories,
we will make one you'll see my love to be true.
Because what I feel cannot be written down
in poetry, prose, or song.

Old Movies And You

I spent most days counting
the days I'd have you near.
I'm not stuck a twenty-one
year old just dreaming
about having a guy like you.
I'm stuck writing poetry
and watching old movies
about the love people had.

I'm like Carole Lombard.
I'm profane but classy.
I know, they know
about me and you
since you made me scream
that day in Scotland.
But I wasn't mad at you,
I was mad at myself
for not letting you in.

You're like Clark Gable.
King of the Silver Screen
and secretly, in love with me.
And love only made me go insane
when it comes down to you
and the stories I've grown fond of.

Stars of the old movies paved a way
for people like us to find a soulmate
to call the one and to waltz with.
But I'm the one to cry over missing you

when our story just barely began.

I'll die like Carole Landis
if things continue on like this.
I don't want to leave the Earth
when I'm stuck singing
the same old tune
about the same old things.
I don't want to be that girl.
I don't want to be without you.

But Old Hollywood Stars,
don't see the world like I do.
They see what they've left.
I see something that's empty,
and sad, and depressing
because you are not in it.

Don't be like Rex Harrison.
To leave me blue is something
you wouldn't be able to do.
It'll leave something bad
in a world that's already broken.

I don't want to be Marilyn Monroe
calling you on the phone for days
just to get torn apart like he did
to me at twenty-two.

I don't want to leave the Earth
hoping that I've made a difference.

I'm just Bonnie Parker
writing down the journey she made
without you by her side.
She's made to make a name for herself
but she's stuck hiding away from the world
because the world feared
the poet who writes about the world
like how she saw it.

But I'm twenty-five and I'm breaking down
out of sight, and lonely.
I know how schedules can be
but busy don't make our bodies
collide like it will in August.

Manila Calling

I never liked traveling to Manila.
It always ends in disaster or tears.
But my father lives there, I don't
want to know what he is thinking.
Maybe he'd let me date you
when he comes around to talk
about why he wouldn't answer
our phone calls for a time.

I never wanted to be in Manila
when everything I ever loved
is in America and London.
I always find joy in calling
you from the phone
and not caring if it's late.
Late doesn't even begin
with how much I love you.

I hear Manila calling for us
to stay apart for quite some time
but I don't want my father to know
that I love a man who lives so far.

Complicated Love

I never liked the sight of couples
holding hands and being in love.
It makes me sick to the bone.
I don't know if it's just me
or how I view the world
but a day of love means nothing.
It all means nothing to me.
I never liked Valentine's Day.
I never saw the point in celebrating love.

But you, you make things complicated.
I love you like I love the stars.
I hate you like the day I screamed.

I never liked Valentine's Day
but you made things different.
You made me believe in love
like I did when I was a child.
Our love is complicated
and people only see
what we want them to see.

I never liked the feeling of being lonely
when it comes to having a romance
in secret and only a few people know.

Babe, you make things complicated.
I know people who are Facebook official.
They make me want to scream
from the top of my lungs,

"I love you! I love you!"
Why is that hard to say?
Why is everything so complicated with you?

But darling, you are a lucky bastard.
You've got a loyalist, a whole hearted girl.
Isn't that better than Valentine's Day?

God Knows

I hear Taylor from the other room.
She's with Joe strumming the guitar
as we're in this empty room fighting.
We haven't seen each other for a long time.
They said to break it up
but we haven't spoken in days.

I can hear his friends in my head.
They're saying that I'm crazy
but God knows I've done nothing wrong.

As I sit in my empty room,
I wonder if silence is a better option
than fighting over nothing.
And God knows, I've tried to find
the words to say to you
but I'm in the state of repeating myself.
I've ran out of words to say to you.
So, I sit here in silence
as you leave the room.
I know, I'm not making it easy for him.

Our Love Is Like A Poem

Our love is like a poem.
There's many lines
that doesn't rhyme
and there are others
that does have sense.
But we've written them down,
for people to read what it's like
to have a love like ours.

And what we do under the sheets,
And the things that we've kept hidden,
will all be there in documentation
for generations to come.

Our love doesn't seek attention
from those who aren't willing
to give love back to those who need it.
But we all need love in hard times.
Though everything we hoped
in a relationship is something
people are still searching for in theirs.

Love Songs And The Blues

There's a lot of love songs
to tell someone you love them.
But those words are someone else's,
still you sing me love songs
on my old red guitar
and in your baritone voice.
You had a bottle of beer
and I had a bottle of Mike's.
It was like the second date
when you sang me the Blues.
Though I requested songs
by George and Ira Gershwin
because I finally found
someone to watch over me.

Music Could

Music could make you lose yourself.
Whether it's the Blues or Jazz,
people get lost by singing songs
that makes them want to fall in love.
There's music to make love to
but we'd never do it to Rhythm and Blues.
Music makes you daydream about
the things that you wanted to happen.
I wish I could get lost in music
like she does and I would love again.
But music is there when you leave,
and you'll leave when things go blue.

I Have Many Flaws

I have many flaws
that I could expose
to a crowd of people
but I don't know
if they'll love me
just the same.

I could write about
a love that only exists
in fairytales
but that doesn't seem
to mend what's been
broken before
you came along.

I don't think that love
could mend anything
that you've broken
from a long time ago.
As I remember it,
you were that boy
who gave so much
of himself to one.
And I did the same.

There are other fishes
that you could catch
in a sea made for men
but I've wondered
why you've decided

to catch me
out of millions of others.

I could be the witch
people wanted to burn
but she couldn't burn.
I could be the Queen
people feared and loathed
because she was destined
to rule over all others.
I could be the artist
who painted a beautiful
portrait of someone
she wanted to be with
for all time.

Like Salt-N-Pepa,
I could talk about
the sex that we did
under bed sheets.
But I'm just a girl
who can run a whole
kingdom with the words
she writes on a page.

There are hearts on a page
that I've written on.
They're all about us
but some about boys
I once loved and admired.
And somehow, I knew
that I'll come back to you.

Blackout

I blacked out not having you around.
I feel ashamed that I have to be
the target of everyone's toxic mess.
Don't they know that I'm just a girl?
And I've got nothing to lose
if I'm just getting started with my life.

I cried the last time I saw you.
No song could describe how I feel
but can she write to you in poetry?
And if I go blonde, will you love me
just the same like you did
when we met in Scotland?

You knew you fucked up
when I told you I didn't care.
But I just wanted you
if my mother weren't around.
You could've told me you love me
and I'd say, "You're crazy."

But it would be a crime,
if people saw you kiss me.
So, you better keep it quiet
when we get a little frisky.
And I'll turn twenty-six,
it'll be my golden day.

I'll blow out the candles
and we could get drunk

with cider and beer
because it would be
deja vu if I'm just
another singer

writing songs about
a love that people dream about.
I've got dreams too.
To be a woman,
loved my millions and no one.
I'm a little selfish.

I get so jealous.
Could you blame me?
I just wanted to be with you
but 2020 makes us believe
in nothing and everything.
I know I can't be in Rome

because that's where you took her
while I was in Spain running around
without a doubt of wanting you.
I blacked out not having you around.
It was sweet hearing you say
that I might be the one for you.

It's all I wanted to hear
someone say to me.
I knew you fucked up
when I walked away
from the sweet conversation
you had with my mother.

But I feel jaded, when things
aren't going my way.
Does she know the way
you speak sounds like a song
from a long time ago?
Because I do, I do, I do.

And if I go blonde,
would you think
that I'm just being rebellious
like how they think of me?
Do they know that the words
they'll speak won't be taken lightly?

I don't want to blackout when it comes
to what we've got going on.
Can we just laugh about the things
we've been through?
Because the past is in the past,
when it comes to those who we used

to love and crave at night.
You know the words I'll write
and you know it's about love.
That's how I feel about you.
That's what I'll say to your face
when I see you again.

I Pray To God

I used to hate what I see.
I didn't like my name
but it's given that I pray to God
to change what I see and hear.
It's a little funny to think
that I have a thing for bad boys
but there's one guy that I love
and he made it good for me
to believe in fairytales again.

And if the other boys I had a crush on
wonders why I believed in them,
I thought they were Romeo
but they're just Tybalt stopping me
for finding who I want to be
and hides the things I wanted for myself.
I pray to God that they see the luck they lost
when they didn't see me for who I was.
Because as tragic as it sounds,
that girl is long gone;
Juliet's in a better place.

I used to hate what I see.
I pray to God that it becomes easy
to be bad but the goodness in me
is breaking apart like the love
I gave to those who never loved me.

I Wrote This About You

I spent days thinking if you meant it
when you said, you love me.
From the very beginning I knew
nothing comes from nothing
if we don't speak up and say the things
that's been in our mind.
So, I picked up a pen
and I wrote this about you
because I know in my heart
that I love you too.

Insanity

Insanity is something women like me
are blamed for but people don't see
the real thing that made us believe.
True, you took her places to forget
the things that made her worry.
But how are you not worried for
the thing that made me who I am?
Darling, I may be insane
but you brought chaos with you.

I'm A Romance Poet

I'm a Romance Poet.
I write about the things
I know of and what I admire
but only from a distance.

I'm a Romance Poet.
I know how to love
like you've never seen.
I'm not a serial dater.
I've never dated anyone
in my life but I played roles
that once tortured me.

I'm a Romance Poet.
I can write for days
about what I wanted.
And I wanted someone
like you in my lifetime.
But it doesn't matter,
now that I've explained
myself to those you wanted
some sort of explanation.

I'm a Romance Poet
but I need to be on the silver screen
in order to fulfill the things
that I've dreamed of as a child.
And I wanted to be loved
like every star that shined
before I came along.

I'm a Romance Poet.
And I don't know when you'll come around
so we can listen to Frank Sinatra
and Bing Crosby and everything
I will introduce you to.
Because I know that time will be
on our side once this torture is over.

I'm a Romance Poet
and there's only one thing
that I want in my life.
And that's you,
no one else but you.

Rendezvous

I've heard from your friends
that you've wanted a life
with a girl that can stand
on the sidelines and smile.
I'm not that kind of girl.
I need sometime to be myself
and to run a business
in order to earn what I desire.

You've sang John Legend
and Bruno Mars just to feel
like you are one with the times.
I'd prefer it if you sang me
the Blues because you make it
worth the listen, my love.
I'm the kind of girl for Jazz
and a little rendezvous
between white sheets
of your hotel room.

We could spend hours
just forgetting about all those people
who wronged us in the past.
Because with you,
the violins will play
a thousand love songs.
And your friends will hear from me
that I only care about the warmth
your arms bring.

I Want To Be The Girl

I am not a girl who knows
everything about a man's world.
I am not a girl who is willing
to be in the sidelines
just for the fun of it.

I am a girl who is willing
to fight and fight
for something that she wants
in her lifetime.
I am a girl who holds her fate
in her own hands
because she can and she will.

It is not terrible to think
of me as dependent
because I only depend on myself.
I just don't want to
walk pretty to the altar.
I want to be the girl
who saved anyone from
the cruel world we live in.

I want to be the girl whose family name
rises from the grave once more.
But we know a woman takes
the family name of a man,
it's what society expects from us.
If I marry you, I don't want to be
the woman who stays at home

all the damn time. And time!
If I marry you, I want to be a part
of something bigger than the two of us.

Belonging

I'm always looking for something
in a relationship that mends
the broken by the hands of a father,
but I always leave at midnight
just so I don't see him acting up.

I'm always looking for someone
who love me like my father did
but men were once boys.
They'll leave you like he left me.

But I'm not Rita Hayworth,
I don't pick up a guitar
and sing out what I'm feeling.
I pick up a pen and write bars
over bars about what I have
trapped inside of me.

I had family members tell me
I don't fit in anymore
when I was born there.
Maybe I'm foreigner,
I speak many different languages
than just my native tongue.
I don't stick around waiting
because I don't need a man
to tell me what I can or can't be.

I feel like I'm losing around
people who once knew me.

I'm not looking for something perfect.
I just want to be in love
with things like I used to.

I used to play the piano
when I was younger.
I had to stop playing
because I wasn't happy
playing the same old tune.

But when I see him there,
I could see someone who won't leave.
And I know I could see myself cry
if he has to go away because of his job,
I might have to stop myself
like I've always done in the past.
I don't want to have to keep on looking
for something that I found in him.

"I belong with him and not to him."
I argue more than I should have.
I don't know if that's just a woman
being hormonal but I never felt
so entitled to say that I have morals.
I have a songbook of memories
just waiting to be sung to a crowd.

If I don't say "I love you"
as often as I should have,
that's only because I know
that he knows I love him
more than I believe in fairytales.

Maybe I've known Cinderella
longer than I've known myself.

I should know who I'm supposed to be
but I feel trapped when I'm without him.
I could love him longer than I want him.
He never said anything bad about
his blonde ex-girlfriend
and her current lover.

I couldn't keep my mouth shut
but I'd rather jump over hurdles
and go through something I've been
broken about. But I know, I got him
since we first met all those years ago.
"Am I just playing myself?"

"Should I keep on writing down
how I'm feeling about the things
I've felt for a long time?"
He could argue with me
but at the end of the day,
who'll be the woman to stay?

I've Made So Many People Mad At Me

I've made so many people mad at me
because I don't want to find something
so proper and unkempt for a job.
Am I too stubborn to be a girl?
I've made plans to write my whole life
and I'm happy just writing out
my feelings out on paper.
They thought that I'd be the girl
for a 9 to 5 but that's not me.

I've made so many people mad at me
because I can write poetry and prose
without having to think about
what it is I'm writing from.
I've written myself an elegy
that could be read when I'm gone.
But I don't want to leave this place
without changing the world
and what society thinks of her.
Am I immature to think that I am not
the woman who could start a change?

I've made so many people mad at me.
I can't be the infamous woman
who wrote about her life
and everything in it that made sense.
I'm always thinking what I can love.
I'm not thinking about the things
other people want from me.
Selfish bitch: I don't think so.

What am I doing wrong
to get people mad at what I do?

I've made so many people mad at me.
Why should it stop when I'm already
at the top of my game?

Sigyn

I'm the wife of mischief
and was taken into his lies.
I had every right to throw every broken
glass that she shattered onto the floor.
I know that it was my doing
that broke the glass in my room
but I had to do it.

Instead of, crying
from the lies
that I encountered
Loki told me.

I took a deep breath
and kept my mind at ease.

I wanted to tell him.
I couldn't tell him
that the vow he took
was forever
and that forever
couldn't last forever
and ever
and ever.

I brushed my tears away
and held my head up high.
I smiled.
"Helpless from what I can feel
but my mind is strong.

I'll find my way knowing
that I'd save myself
from another broken vow."

He took a deep breath
and said "darling,
you are the mere reason why
I resist the urge to seek another
for my infidelity that broke my heart."

"How do I know that's what you mean?"
My heart frayed
but I stopped it from shattering
into a million little pieces
"How do I know that's what you mean?
How do I know that's what you mean?"

Eliza Hamilton

You wrote me letters
that I read at night.
It kept me sane
while waiting for you
to stay alive.
I wore pastel blue
to match your eyes.
I gave you all my love
without asking questions.
You had your redemption
but I was mortified
with what you've done.

You wrote about her
in time, in doubt.
You thought it wouldn't
reach me but it did
and it broke my heart
knowing that you could
do that to us.
I burnt all the letters
that could've seen
your redemption.
Because you broke my heart,
you broke it in two,
and it could never be put back
in the same way.

The narrative was clear
but my mind was timeless.

In my final hours,
you were always in my mind.
I spent my days explaining
your story to the world
when I could've been writing mine.
I want you to know
that I love you more than
what the world brought to light.
I ask you in my final hours
what shade of pink
will take me towards
the finish line.

Save Me The Waltz

Save me the waltz
and everything will be fine
between me and you.
The fear of losing you
will be nothing compared
to the death of a friend.

I never wanted to dance
without you by my side.
I'm selfish, I know
but all I want is time
with my lover.
Pastel pink dresses

and Shakespeare on the television.
We played Jazz on the radio.
We got lost in the moment.
You said, "save me the waltz"
and I will only if you promise me
that I'm the only one.

How Could You?

How could you leave me?
I'm not the girl you wanted
that's what I get out of you.
You left me broken.
You left me bruised.
The fight isn't enough
but you left me stranded
and home alone.
How could you do that
to someone you love so dearly?
You left me hurting.
You left me thinking
this love isn't worth the fight.
I love you too much
maybe that's my downfall.
I hope arsenic is enough
for me to let you go
as red wine is spilled
on the kitchen floor.
Twenty-five, home alone.
How could you leave me so easily
and not say a single goodbye?
You left me hurting.
You left me hurting.
How could you do that
to someone who loves you?

Timeless

Sylvia Plath once said
"a future was lost yesterday"
and it's true. Losing something
without a doubt of feeling
the way we feel can be
an unbreakable haven.

I know this summer
would be cruel without you.
I kept so many secrets
from my family but I wish
they knew what you are to me.
Dirty jokes floods the room

with laughter and joy.
But so close to you
is where I want to be.
I don't want to get lost
with the times
when you are not around.

I want to be timeless
being in love with you.
No, I don't want to seek
attention every time
we're in public.
The haunting of my heart saying,

"I don't want to lose you."
Time seems to fade away

when we have another.
I don't want anyone else
if the candlelight is all
we've got to light up the room.

High on the wire
walking slowly
as we realize we've got
nothing to lose
when it comes to love.
I got scared of the view.

I saw monsters in the ocean.
I lost the blues when it comes
down to what's real.
Neon pink ashes as we found
each other in bad times.
I don't know if what's better

when it's been all about you.
I was happier before the real you
came along and destroyed me.
"I don't want to lose you"
echoes in my mind
as you went back to her.

Manhattan's pastel pink skies
is all that we saw burning bright.
I honored you and bless my heart.
We fought before you said,
"you are the only one."
I want to be timeless with you.

Spend My Life With You

I want you to know
it's been you all my life.
You've been the boy
in my wildest dreams.
I don't know why things
in my dreams comes true.
You in my highlight reel
since December of last year.

I want to spend my life with you
even if it means dying without you.
We've shared so many things
that made me realize
you had me at seventeen.
It scared me but only for a few days.
The injustice of people who never
knew what it's like to be me.

Homecoming Queen most days
but I've never got my crown
or been told I deserved my titles.
I cried for you, not at you.
I want to spend my life with you.
I don't want to be without you.
I'm the one who stayed
while others leave you alone.

You bring out the better in me.
Rose gold cellular devices
and melted butter on the table.

The smell of coffee coming
from your home office.
Me wanting you from the other side.
I know. You've been the boy
in my wildest dreams.

I don't want to lose
that kind of person. And love,
true love is something
people wish for but never gotten.
They live carelessly through others
with such passion and livelihood.
And love songs makes things worse
for people like me to end up alone.

The Politicians

Growing up surrounded by politicians
is something the world seems to imply
onto women like me but it's nothing
in the world of someone trusting.
I've been through and had enough
of the corruption politics has on me.
All the scandals I've known about
as a child of the nineties.
It's barely anything if you stood
beside the devils of the crimes.

Granddaughter of a President
who gave out speeches
for those she governed and trusted.
Made a friend of a former foe
because of what she knew about
every past lover a politician has.
Never used it to threaten their livelihood
but used it to defend myself
and everything I've done in the past.
I know nothing and everything
all at once but I've never been the one to fall.

Since December, I knew that one day
it will all come back and haunt them.
All the lies. All the torturous crimes.
Spanish lullabies and iridescent colors
making its way out of the bluest ocean.
Crazy feelings and deafening noises.
Should I know where I stand

when I've been made speechless before?
Democratic rights and those wearing red
to a funeral of a forgotten hero.

I don't know if the young knows
when to run around and say,
"It's my time to save people
from the ruthless game of politicians."
I'm left surrounded by those who thinks
romantic orientation is a fad that will fade.
I know myself and who I am going to become.
Counting the days for when people will get
the final portrait I've painted at eighteen.
How much will it cost for everything to be alright?

Lovers And Strangers

Passion is worth the second look.
It's in every book you've read
before you told every lie in the book.
You've committed to acting
like an infamous stranger
drifting over a stream of nothingness.
I always wanted to feel something
when I've had enough of not being
the girl you always wanted.

I should've read the signs
and never came back to you.
You never loved me like I loved you.
I might've missed the red flags
that waved at me when it came with you.
The rarity of keeping you close
was something that made me cry.
I'm hurting the same way
you've been hurting.

Only the likes of you who kept me
from running into someone else's arms.
I don't want to live childless
when it comes down to our demise.
I'm the victim of your downfall.
I'm not the one who was willing
to commit a crime and have an affair.
I'm innocent of the things
you've accused me of.

Twenty-two years old filled with hope
and the mistress of being wronged
by the one she loved and loved.
Take a look at the book I've left behind.
The stories you told your new girl
about me are all false accusations.
Please, believe me when I say,
"you are the only one who can stay"
except you betrayed me by not loving me.

I've never fought for myself
when you belittled me with words.
I've burned brighter than the world
and the things moments fade into.
A damned witch in your eyes
but I seek nothing than to be good.
We must've been in better hands
before we held each other close
and I shed the tears I cried.

Twisted Cruelty

A twist in fate that changes into something
better than what we've got buried underneath.
Teenage dreams coming truthfully.
I don't regret all the guys I've dismissed
and disposed of because it led me to you.
I knew of cities cruel than a villain,
more deafening than a sorceress' scream.
I knew how I ran when I was younger.
Looking back at everything I've done.
I don't regret every word I've said.
Though in twisted reality I loved and left.
Aimed higher than what other girls
wanted to have in their lifetime.
As a child, I wanted the Zac Efron type
but he was brutal and cruel to give love to.
I never knew I wanted the sensible guy
to make a house a home for a girl like me.
They all tried to dispose of me
when I was twenty-two and naïve.
I was the flame they tried to put out.
Curiosity never killed me. It's something
that made me who I am and I love that
fact about the things that made me whole.

Voices, Pt. 2

I heard your voice among the others
that seemed to burn me alive.
Come to me and tell me
I'm not crazy to listen to voices
like the ones in my head.

When breaking up was easy,
I listened to what other people
keeps on telling me to do.
Forever seems like a fantasy
with the people I've listened to.

Your voice was the one thing
that held me closer to the end.
It made me cry knowing
we couldn't have what we wanted.
But it makes me wonder,

if things were different to begin with.
All the voices in my head
repeating the same things
I've heard what you said to my face.
You strummed my red guitar

just to change the conversation.
You knew I didn't like to talk
about the things I've done
in the past with other boys.
Starry skies in the night

and pastel pink jumpers
to keep the cold out the door.
Strawberry ice cream
with two silver spoons.
It was a way to keep

San Francisco Bay colder
than Chicago in your eyes.
Could I hear a much better man?
They're just voices anyway
nothing more than just a voice

for me to listen to
whenever I'm lost at sea.
But the voices destroyed
the person I was before
you came into the picture.

The voices tend to linger
on and on about the things
I never wanted for myself.
I'm an actress but not the one
you see on the silver screen.

I'm an actress whose voice
gets muted by the men
that surrounds her.
I held back my power
because I thought

that's what the people wanted
from a girl like me.

But out of the ordinary,
I saw a phoenix ready
to take flight once again.

Wild, Pt. 2

I'm not a demon for running
with the wolves every full moon.
I'm not a wicked witch
for casting a spell on the man
who loves me more than I do.

I'm like a wild animal
but only by choice.
I gather what I can find
most harvest days.
American stories

made to sing out
in the open but it doesn't
end on a light note
like every animated fairytale.
Punctured and bruised

by stupid games.
It wasn't played by children.
They were played by adults
behaving like children.
I'm not a girl to gossip

about who's sleeping with who
because I've been on the receiving
end of being called a wild spinster.
Wild things can get what they wanted
but it doesn't mean it's fixed.

People get burned alive
once they get compared
to someone they know
nothing about.
For me, I wanted

to be like the graceful
women of the past.
They were wild and exotic
to wide eyed girls
who wanted to be seen.

I've known wilder things
than people using metaphors
at me thinking that I would
get what they mean by it.
But to hell to the wild girl,

she got what she deserved.
Lonely and wild spinster.
That's all that she is, right?
Wrong. I'm more than that.
I'm a poet with a degree

in a circus full of lion tamers.
Women being the lion.
They end up getting hurt
and called out for a crime
they didn't commit.

American folklore about the past.
It made me think twice

about writing things I've been through.
Cautious without an armor.
I'm not made to have new beginnings

once I've been hit in the heart
with the last silver bullet.
I know I'm not a woman
of the past but why do I keep
on wanting a life like theirs?

I did have wild times
and wild predictions
of where I'll end up.
But the reality is,
I'll only end up hurting

the one who loves me.
I'm not the innocent girl
people think I am.
I've held the burden
of knowing he'll stay.

To think about it,
I should be happy
knowing that what I have
in life is there for a reason.
I left poverty and hopelessness

in my place of birth.
I wasn't the first world girl
who writes poetry endlessly.
I was the girl who got her start

by accident because he couldn't

keep it quiet.
That's what's wild about him.
He's not afraid to scream
out a name endlessly.
I'm wild enough to love him.

Skin, Pt. 2

Lasting tender touches
on my skin left me feeling
weak and lost in lust.
I can feel you getting under
my bridges as I held my body up
while losing myself

in your gorgeous blue eyes.
Kiss me softly
but don't stop tangling
your fingers in my hair.
Let's let the shower
fall on us like raindrops.

Make me say it.
Make me scream it.
I know I want you
all to myself
but just looking at you
the words comes out

like gibberish
and not English.
Kiss me all over my skin
but leave me wanting more
if you can lead me there.
Press your body against mine

and don't let the blues
take me far away

from your fingertips.
Make me purr like a kitten
seeking for a brand new
adventure to take.

Hit me. Shake me.
But playfully and out of love.
They don't have to know
that you were with me
the day before my birthday.
Don't let a teardrop fall

easily right down my cheeks
as we get lost in a warm embrace.
My tears are the reason
why I lay awake at night.
I know I couldn't bear to seek
what I've hoped for

just to leave me in my skin.
Kiss me sweetly. Kiss me quickly.
You know I love you.
It's there suggestively
as we lay in my bed
with nothing on.

Complicated, Pt. 2

It was a Monday.
I was first on the list
and the first to arrive.
I was first to lose my mind
but between the two of us:
it wasn't an act.
I wanted for others
to hear my cries.
But I didn't know
you fell in love with me,
I know I'm complicated
and there's nothing going on
inside my mind.

But I'm not sorry for crying,
I wanted to change your mind
about not wanting to be
with someone like me.
I dared to spend so much
on nothing because I break
things so easily.
I'm not the perfect angel
people make me out to be.
I'm just the complicated
little girl from years ago.

To tell you the truth,
a heart like mine
is meant to be broken
before I gets healed

by your hands
if that's what it's supposed
to be with us.

But from what I know,
love is complicated
nothing is ever perfect.

Touch, Pt. 2

Festival lights gracing the sky.
Christmas songs playing
on the radio like I've never left
this charming, beautiful country.

Hated how I left turning my back
on something I knew but I guess,
people do to the innocent ones.
Hated the bittersweet times

I wanted to come back
to the girl I once was
but I love who I became.
The parol's high in the sky

like the star of David.
But what I loved most
about my homeland
is the touch of the sun.

I want you there with me
all Christmas season.
We could walk down
Manila Bay and forget

about the deadlines
we have to make.
Even if you have to turn
down something you've been

dreaming of all your life
just so you could be with me.
Hold me on my grandmother's sofa.
I never had enough of the way

you smell like sunlight.
It's a little out of touch
for some people who doesn't know
the things we do at night.

Two different people can never be
the same in a world of blasted hopes.
Hated being called a foreigner
by the people I grew up with

as a young girl.
I don't speak in my native tongue
anymore but you should know
how much I wanted to keep

talking to my family
even if they don't see me
as a native of the country.
But it's your touch

that brings me back home
to the little house in Fairwoods
my mother wanted to pass on
to my sister and I.

And I can't handle the things
I left because they don't

define who I became.
Stars aligned on my way

to America from London.
I remember falling for the city
and a ferris wheel
many tourists ride every time they come.

I felt like it was home
but I know I never could stay.
Friday night out of town
like I've always been.

I know there's something
about your touch
that brings me back home
to the places I once left.

I ran away from home
every time I see darkness
but you bring a touch
of light into gray skies.

I'm always the one
who has the perfect diction
in the English language
in my family.

My mind isn't in the perfect state
but I can find love stronger
than any drug I can get addicted to.
I know something about addiction

and gamboling my life away
like my father did with money.
I couldn't forgive what happened
but I can make a new life

with the words I write.
But that doesn't come close
on the way you touch me
in the dark of the night.

Closure, Pt. 2

Don't stand too close
or I'll scream out loud.
Don't stand so far
or I'll end up missing you.
Don't leave me without
any closure from this
God damn cruel casualty.

You did some hurtful
things just to get
my full attention.
I don't care about
being alone again.
Boys just make me cry
and make me think

I'd rather be alone.
All my life I've been searching
for closure away from you
but my heart knows
what I needed and wanted.
It's you. That's the closure
I've always been looking for.

Signs in empty spaces.
Beyond the bright lights
of the city I've loved and left.
I've been an immigrant
twice in my life
but born into a year

people seem to push away.

Never gotten the love I wanted
but love was something I had.
It surrounded me in my life.
Sweeter than fiction
but love is a ruthless game
when you always win
in a fight that never got old.

Closure. Closure. Closure.
I've been looking for that
the whole time I've been around.
Seventeen years of searching
for something that never gotten
into the lights of the world.
But my love for you,

should it be carefree
is up to the places you take me to.
Whether it's Paris or Rome,
I just want to be with you.
Hold me close and never let me go.
Because you know, I wanted you
since I was twenty-one.

Carole Landis

I'm screaming, "Rex, please,
stay by my side for the night
and no one has to know."
But he didn't listen,
I kept on begging for him
to stay, stay, stay.

It was hopeless to cry
but I had to cry to myself.
Took the last bottle of champagne
and the pills to help ease the pain
but it was no use.
I couldn't help but think to myself.

What have I done wrong
that he would leave me for her?
She may be his wife
but I've got my life.
Dear God, I know I'm hopeless
when it comes to love

but I promise I'll be better
when I leave this place.
It's torture to my heart
to see him with someone else
much wiser than I could be.
And yet, I'm the icey blonde

in an equation of love.
Blank spaces beside my name

as I spend this night alone.
I wish that it was easy
to be in love with someone like him
but it's not. It's a tragedy.

A life for a wife
and a happy marriage.
If I'm called the home wrecker
in this Greek tragedy. I'm out.
I don't want to be know
for ruining a marriage like theirs.

I just want to be loved
by someone who cares about me.
I'm not sorry for saying
that this is goodbye.
I have to go away, far from here
if it's going to be this way.

Homeland

I don't hate my homeland
but I've been gated all my life
wondering if I'll ever come back
wanting people to love me for who I am
not for the color of my skin.

Part Spanish but I don't speak
a word of my native tongue
because of what other people
might say behind my back.
I wonder if the white lies

of a nation will always haunt
my daydreams of becoming
someone I wanted to become.
I'm not Benedict Arnold.
I won't turn my back on

the things I once knew.
It feels like a tango
of something to reclaim.
I want my own voice
to be heard by millions.

I don't care if I get hated
but the universe knows me.
No one's purely an angel.
We don't play the same tunes
on the radio once we get the chance.

I fell in love with the glitz
and the glamor of my days in the sun.
I don't want to start over
when it comes to my cultural being.
I strayed away from the darkness

once it caught a friend of mine.
I never befriended someone
of the same ethnicity as mine.
Lonely when it comes to those
who surrounds her.

Broken once about the things
I'm not sorry about what I said.
I don't hate my homeland
but I've never felt the royalty
people say foreign ones get treated.

I guess they wanted a Benedict Arnold
to speak her mind and turn her back
on a world she once knew.
My homeland is not where unicorns
fly over and over every time

I wanted to speak.
Silence by what she knows.
I can't just say nothing
to anyone but my mind
will tell you you're wrong.

I love my homeland
but don't say you treat

people like me like royalty
when all you see is people
wanting you to fail and fail again.

The Icy Blonde

Skin deep burned in the past.
Iron lady in the back of the club,
the girl doesn't want to show
all the darkness that overpowers.

She's been called the icy blonde
by dozens of people behind her back.
She was young and in love
that made her a fool without gold.

"Don't worry, baby," she says
as she looked at herself in the mirror.
Things will be different the next time
you find yourself singing an old song.

She wants to be happier with him
than be alone in the world.
Good girl never spoken against
the people who belittled her.

Her heart wants her to stay
but her mind was made up.
She saw the gray skies
aligning with the pastel pink sunset.

Lusting in his beauty
but she doesn't want to be the girl
who saw him with another.
Darling girl, don't leave just yet.

There will be plenty of fish
to catch in the ocean.
Love the way you reclaim
your name and give the people

what they don't want.
Your heart is stronger
than anything you've been through.
The world will be lonely

without you and I hope you see it.
She's the icy blonde in tales
people tell each other.
Real girls gets stranded

in an island alone
even if we knew the last thing
she wanted to have.
It was him. It's been him all along.

Sunday Evening

Sunday evening,
we packed our bags
just to leave for the city.
I thought it would be
the last thing we do.
I don't want you to leave
for Prague and Rome.

Sunsets and walks on the beach.
I remember you doing the same
thing with your ex-girlfriend.
We're not the same girl.
We don't like the same things.
But we think for each other,
deja vu is not something you wanted.

I wanted us to tour the city.
Finding new things to do together
without the need of open skies
and the summer heat.
It doesn't have to be on our itinerary.
But babe, we could be sharing
a glass of milkshake under the Californian sun.

New England chowder in the pot
as I turned on the radio.
My hips and your strength above me.
We contributed to the glory
of one night together alone.
Just one night without fighting

with each other like we've done before.

Keep the bright lights of the city
outside while you send me over the edge.
Can you feel my heart beating fast?
Our idols were at war before we seen
the last of the noises people make.
You understand me that's all I need
from a love like this.

Beautiful People

Beautiful people has something
in their grasps that I always wanted.
Fortunate girls without the burden
of being called foreign by family.
Don't ask me why I'm alone
every Tuesday night
or why I don't window shop
whenever I feel lonely.

I'd rather be like Anne Boleyn.
Carefree and ahead of her times.
But beautiful people has something
everyone wanted to have.
I just want a fate that makes me
bigger than I am now.
Scary things that make us human.
But I'm building a bigger castle,

for me as a shelter from all the ruthless
games people play with me as the pawn.
I've got pride but that's what killed me.
I don't want to live like everyday
is a fight to survive a battle.
Beautiful people can say things
they want to say but it never takes a toll
on their livelihood.

But I'm not one of them.
Because whatever I say,
it comes around to haunt me.

I don't want that.
I don't want something
to burn me alive
like the things burning
every moment I have alone.

Ghost

I'm like a ghost in his mind.
He can't seem to let me go.
I've been burned in his head
to be like you in a way
of a girl wondering around
with a new boyfriend.

I'm not seeing a bigger stance
on how much men are in control
but I'd rather be the one
in control of my own destiny.
He has me hidden away
and trapped like I've always been.

I've had my fair share of disruption
against all the odds spoken against me.
But still I linger on in his mind
like an old song people sang,
a jukebox made to sing out loud.
I'm not going around being another girl

just so they can take me
and burn me alive.
They'll make me feel like a sinner
rather than a saint.
I don't want to be the ghost
of the past that haunts him.

We both know he'd rather
have a girl who's faithful and loyal.

I don't know if I could be that girl
he wanted to spend his life with.
I'm a little boring but I can write
a little melodic rhythm

to the blues I've been feeling
since he's been out of town.
I know we both saw glittering pink lights
when he graces the silver screen
like he's a mixture of Clark Gable
and Errol Flynn.

I don't want to be a ghost
in the back of his mind
from a long time ago.
I don't want to see him
due because of me.
I know I've killed him

by not loving him from the start.
I can't remember when the candlelight
was at its dimmest speck.
It makes no sense to me
that I'd be the one to haunt you.
But fragile things tend to disappear

within the reach of one man.
Can't he tell I'd rather be the girl
who sees the better in him?
I want to see my Robin Hood
save me from myself
once my reputation grows cold.

Hurting Me

I spent years buried
in hundreds of thorns
as a halo above my head
but I was never the one
to face the truth from the lies
I've been told by my elders.

I guess I seem to be the reason
why everyone backs out of being
wholesome and pure hearted.
But still I'm simulated in situations,
I never wanted to be in.
To tell you the truth,

I used to fill my head with the lies
others told me in the past.
But my kindness has the better of me,
and to be fair and true is something
I'm still learning and becoming.
I won't sugar coat the things

people wanted me to know as a child.
But it's in my adolescence that I learned
so many bad things about life.
Professors won't see me at my best
that's what I told myself as a teen.
I wish guys like Dillon would see

the scarification made by women
from many, many, many generations.

But he's too prideful, too selfish
to understand why I kept quiet
while he belittled me in front
of all of our peers.

He took my rightfully earned crown
but that's alright by me.
I have someone else willing to listen
without me having to ask for his time.
Dillon, he lost my respect
when he told the world

of all of my faults.
I want to bid him farewell
but his anger was too loud
from him to hear my goodbye.
Changed his name on the internet
to Chase Graves thinking

that I wouldn't know.
Hardheaded, shallow minded
neurotypical boy who promised the world
but he thought it's over for a girl like me.
I still got a long list of gentlemen
to speak my mind to.

I guess that I'll have to start with him.
His heart heart his filled with anger
but I'm the one who turned so blue
by keeping my mouth shut.
I only spoke kindly to his face.
I never said things to hurt him

but why does he want to hurt me?
A little battle between the sexes
is something that he wanted.
He is dignified with torture
and violent delights
but he won't write a single

lullaby just to calm himself to sleep.
I guess that he'll have to keep
an eye on the clock
and into the soul of another girl
if that's what he wanted
out of his dreadful war he started.

The Death Of Me

Somber lullabies and twinkling lights
above me in the night's sky.
Changed my last name
when I signed my heart away.
White dress and red roses
keeps me guessing what I would be
without him by my side.

I would feel like Carole Landis
when Rex Harrison broke her heart.
My mind will numb the pain I'm feeling.
Fluorescent lights and the Doctor
saying that I'll live through
the rebirth of snakes in the air.
Fluttering in the wind

while I say my vows
that I wrote on my own.
Love, loving him in the future tense.
I brought myself to imagine
a life without him right there
but I just couldn't.
It's death that holds me close

whenever I feel numb.
It's not around the corner
but why do I keep on looking there?
There must be some somber feeling
that I missed while listening
to a friend's reclaimed lullabies

on my smart phone late at night.

I feel like Carole Landis most days.
Faking smiles and forcing laughter.
In my head that sounded like a melody
but it never could be created
in a way that feels like a broken record.
Ten minutes into a novel
I borrowed from him a long time ago.

Never returned it but I'm sure
I won't miss it as the book
contains photographs of the past.
I was seven when I first met him.
He told me his name but I didn't care.
I know it hurt him to see me
like an open wound that didn't heal.

I promise when I walk down
in a white dress with my brother
walking by my side
I won't turn a blind eye
on the things that made
everything lined up so perfectly.
We won't be a perfect couple

but that won't matter
when I have him to myself
all throughout the nights
will have together.
And yet, the death of me
will be his only weakness.

I won't go before he does.

That's a promise to all
who knows what keeps my mind
at ease when it comes to true love.
I guess the white dress
and the pink satin sash will have to wait
until I'm ready to face the world
with him as my man.

Love Is A Desperation

I wish it was easy to be with you
but I'm desperate to be loved by you.
It seems a little monstrous to end
the day without seeing you in the view.

I'm broken but to the sound of silence.
I saw you there with a gleam
in your deep blue eyes
and the Clark Gable way about you.

I'm not a broken record
but I'd rather spend a day alone with you
right there to hold me.
There's a sincere allowance to love you

in the depths of the dark.
It's cinegraphical when it comes
to romance with love and lust.
You had me at hello

but I don't want you to know that.
I wanted you to keep on guessing
whether I love you or not.
I guess we were both desperate

of the other's company for a time
until we can nurture the torture
time had on us but we feel
like we have to obey the rules.

With you, I want to bend everything.
I want to see the world with you there.
It'll be like a wondrous time
with french champagne at an occasion.

Was it a mistake for me to love you?
We're not in a love story.
This isn't a Shakespearean fairytale.
It's a small town with the twinkling lights of the city.

We're desperate to spend a day
fiddling with the clowns in the circus.
Je t'aime de tout mon coeur, mon coeur…
I love you with all my heart, my heart

is fragile and altered to fit in with the times.
But I don't feel as free as I should be.
Let me be the first to control my own destiny
like I've done when I was younger.

The burning desire and the desperation
we both went through as fallen foes.
I wish it was easy to be in love with you.
We fought most days but I'm burning

without knowing how it'll affect
the version of me you saw.
Romeo, save me from the desperation I feel.
I know I'm not Juliet but I'm an inch away

from the Lord's grasp of my soul.
Broken hearts mended by time.

I don't know the cause I've craved
since I left the boy next door

for the one I truly love.
Moon over water and ocean.
I want to spend my days with you
right there to hold me.

I'm in love with the one
who came into my life time and time again.
I'm never the beautiful one
or the homecoming queen.

I always leave the party
when it gets interesting.
I never wanted to dance alone
in the crowd of thousand faces.

I want so much just to be with you.
The view up here is dimming my light
but what the hell am I missing?
Other boys seems to turn a blind eye

on being with a loyalist like me.
I'll never hurt anyone who cares about me.
I couldn't change the girl they saw.
I know she just wants a love that's pure and magical.

Rendezvous, Pt. 2

Don't pretend like we haven't
thought of a rendezvous
between the sheets like we're the stars
of our own little movie.

Changed the facts into fiction.
I'm not destined to be a bride
that's what they keep on telling you
while you went around being Clyde

to a musician's Bonnie Parker.
I never wanted to be Cinderella
but I guess that's all I will be
when it comes to loving you.

I want to be alone in a room
with you tangling your fingers
in my dark, dark hair.
If it's rendezvous we'll know,

it'll be something worth it.
But am I worth the pain?
Look me in the eyes
and tell me I'm like royalty.

Don't lose yourself
in this rendezvous.
We won't be the bright star
everyone wanted out of me.

I can't even hold a job
like how the others do.
Be humble, that's what they tell me.
Be a common woman

everyone wants but I know
I couldn't be that girl.
I have a purpose to be
someone I wanted to become.

Listen to me roar like a lion
in the dark when it comes
to the sorry feeling we feel.
Beautiful tunes of the radio

coming closer to mend the sky.
I want you to hold me in the dark
when it comes to spending a night
between the sheets with you.

We've done some foul things
in our youth that came back
and haunted us like we were prey.
I don't want to burn

like a flicker of a candle.
I'm a mess when it comes to love.
Born in 1981 and I was born in 1995.
People seem to crave the passion we've got.

I know I don't need saving
when it comes to the indolence

I feel like a common woman.
But I'm not common,

I love being insane
and feeling tense between two people.
I'm not a princess
but I'll be your princess,

I'll be your princess.
Not that it matters
but a little rendezvous is all we need
to make use of the time we've got.

Pretending

Silver skyline, Nineties rap music,
Will Smith's Miami blasting
from my computer speakers.

Happiness doesn't want us
to pretend we're flying.
It keeps us buried in the sand.

But sandcastles is all we can build,
the world doesn't know brown eyes
is quite the burden when it comes

to our romantic orientation
because sexuality is all
that the world knows.

They don't see the things
we have fallen for.
2Pac's Dear Mama is playing

whenever we feel alone
and we've got nothing to spare.
Bad kids club is all we'll know

if we don't send each other
a little bouquet of flowers.
Sixteen years old,

I wish you knew the darkness
I felt when you said I couldn't be

the girl for you.

I appreciate you coming
to the small party.
It wasn't a night to remember

but I remember is like
it was yesterday.
Happiness is something

we wanted to feel.
But it's all that we wanted,
I know how tears fall.

I know how it makes us believe
in something we don't want.
I wanted to be with someone

who cares so much about me
than I could ever do for myself.
Eighteen years old,

I wanted to erase your name
from my crimson lips.
But something wanted us,

to be the people who becomes friends
even if we have to pretend
that nothing's wrong.

I Wish You Knew

I wish you knew
how much hurt
I've been through.
I wanted a friend
who would care
about the things
I'm going through.

I guess you're just like
the rest of them.
You want me to burn.
You want me to fail.
But Social Media got us,
falling in love with words
and embracing what others

see in the both of us.
I wish you knew
how you changed
by the things we loved.
OPM music and the nineties
banging through the speakers.
But how I loved you is way different

than the love I feel for him.
When will we burn
the town like we've done
before we saw each other.
Just around and date
other girls like you've always done.

I won't be hurting

because people think of me
as the side chick no one
knows a lot about.
I wish you knew
how that will hurt me.
I just wanted a friend
who would hold my hand

in the dark of the night.
Two Social Media stars
wanting nothing to do
with the pain of others
but we get dragged
by the hurt they feel.
We wonder if it was our fault

that they're lives are at risk.
Red lipstick on the coffee cup
you've kept when we last saw each other.
He doesn't have to know
about the friends we've got
and the things we've never done.
Let them speculate

and slut shame the girl
who wanted nothing
but to be loved and loved.
Isn't it unfortunate
that we're the pair
most likely to succeed

in the field we burned?

I wish you knew
I was the one
who wanted space
and I thought you wanted it too.
Let me be the first
to apologize for not seeing it through.
I wish it was different

but we can't let the birds
tell our lovers what we've done
to each other's game plans.
Just let them know
what they wanted to know,
nothing, nothing ever happened
between us that summer.

A Version Of Me

There's a little of what I know
out there in the world.
I'm not the shining star
people think of when they see you.

A version of what they knew
is something to reconsider
when it comes down to change.
Red wine spilled on the floor.

Showing what comes naturally.
And something is different,
bold, and stronger than a drug.
Never spoken to anyone

about our love but I guess
It's dangerous to be hopeful
as a woman these days.
It'll be better if I were

soft spoken and useless.
I wanted nothing more
than to be with someone
who loves me truly.

What do I have to gain?
What do I have to feel?
Am I just a robot
who has to feel ashamed?

Nothing is ever wrong
to feel like you don't belong.
I felt like a sinner
all my life but with him

things are different.
He makes me feel
like a princess
without a crown.

I Fancy You

I think there's a reason
why we met that summer
in Edinburgh, Scotland.
I fancied you knowing
we couldn't be together.
Love is forbidden
and angers the rest.

Why is it so easy
to be with you
when I was born
to be a spinster?
And yet, fancy things
is something I admired
growing up in the suburbs.

But falling is something,
I've done in my life.
No one to catch me
so I ended up being
the girl who was never
rescued by a man
who failed to notice

her only wish was to love him.
You don't have to be a prince
to know what a woman wants.
A woman wants her freedom
but never a day to cause
others pain and suffering.

I fancy you a lot.

That's the only thing
that cause me so much pain
to a woman like me.
Loving someone
so fragile and careful.
I love you with all
that I have in me.

That summer in Edinburgh
was a taste test
of the things we can
go through in one day.
I fancy you from
the very beginning.
I guess I was too afraid to show it.

Little Butterfly

I wanted so little
than what I've got.
You can thank
your lucky stars
about the things
we've done without
the other fallen
for the things
I've seen with my eyes.

Butterflies seems to come
over me when it comes
to you and I alone in the sun.
Russian poets seems
to scatter in the ocean
without you there.
Protect me was all I ever
gotten from the boys
who wanted a lady.

I'm sure they were only
desperate for a lover
under the covers of their bed.
They've flown miles over me.
But I'm still grounded,
I'm still the same girl
who wanted the best for her.
Call me a bitch.
Call me a devil.

I've been called worse
than you can ever say.
Little butterflies
is all I could ever feel
with the courage
of missing you.
I love you with all
of my being.
I hope we'll fly together.

Loving You

Loving you makes me feel insane.
I don't know whether to hate you
or to kiss you at certain times.

I'm hurting when you cry and argue
with me and you know I'm someone
from the first day we met many years ago.

I hate to say it but I wanted to be the one
who wanted to see the sights.
I guess things had to happen to us

on that very day we met.
The people who knew me
knows I'm kind of shy.

But with you, it's different.
I can freely speak my mind
and dispose of the burden placed upon me.

Loving you is worth my time.
I must admit I've never saw myself
with someone like you before.

I've hurt myself not knowing if the times
were against something so pure like love.
I've jumped over a few hurdles in my time

but I've never flown higher than the skies.
I know that happiness is a virtue

everyone's been seeking in a lifetime

but I've got it and it's with you.
Because loving you is something
I would do until my dying day.

Mistake

Mistakes were made when you showed
the real you to everyone in the room.
Selfish and careless with a breakable heart.
I wish you wouldn't tell everyone
that it was me who changed everything.
I'd rather not be the one who takes and takes.
I'd rather be the girl who wins in something
she's destined to become.

It was a mistake to love you
even though you made a fool
out of the girl you're with.
She believed in everything
and in nothing like it was her true calling.
But passion is something
that you are lacking, my friend.
It feels as if you are a robot
who is ashamed to let go of the past.

I have wasted my time claiming
that you can be someone
who can sit on a throne.
You lied your way to the top
while I'm still lingering in the dark.

Selfish boy,
I hope you understood
why I'll never respect
a dying wish like the one
you made to me

when I wasn't looking.
I'm ashamed to call you
an old friend
because of the path you've made.

You've Made A Fool Out Of Me

You've made a fool out of me
when you became the man
you said you wouldn't become.

You've made a fool out of me
when you became reckless
and down-right rude.

You've made a fool out of me
when you said that I was the one.
I wish you didn't say it just to keep me.

I wish you didn't make a fuss
out of wanting to have me.
You've made it difficult for me

to realize that I could be someone.
You've made a fool out of me
when you told me to look into your eyes

and I lost myself in them.
I wonder if you knew the power
you have over me with those eyes of yours.

Green eyes makes a girl feel
envious of the power it has.
But I've fooled myself

by believing in you
and your cruel ways

that held onto this fragile heart of mine.

Landslide

I brought myself to disappear
once or twice in my life
but I never wanted the landslide
to happen to anyone else.

I know how much I wanted
was something I never had
to defend and tolerate.
You said love has always been

the same as it always has been.
But why am I feeling like a clown?
Why am I becoming someone
I never wanted to become one?

I've been fooled by you
and your ocean blue eyes.
It is in my honest being
that I fell in love with you.

But why do I feel like I'm falling
past the mountains and into a pit?
Even though you love me,
we're not like Romeo and Juliet.

We are not from duelling households.
We tend to find comfort in each other
without the violent tastes of the sun.
We're not a landslide fallen over head.

But I wanted to be with you.
Is it a crime to want you?
Is it a crime to be the girl
you've always wanted?

I loved you since I was seventeen
but my heart seemed to wonder.
And I hurt you by doing so.
I'm sorry. I'm sorry. I'm sorry.

The Harder We Fall

The harder we fall, the faster we run.
I bet you tell that to the other girls
you've been with before me.
We've been around the world
but nothing seems to fit with
the version of our love.

I bet you'd rather run away
with the next girl you see.
I'm not that kind of girl
so you better look elsewhere
for someone who'd run a mile
without the pressures of perfection.

Knowing that I'm just another
wide eyed girl you'll walk past
is a little to fitting for the world
we both live in. Don't you think?
The world seems to be far more
greater than the both of us.

The harder we fall, the faster we run.
It seems to be the mantra of the season.
Forgetting the past to make room
for the newer rendition of an old song
we used to play during a heatwave.
Five years ago, in July was when she had you.

You could've been with me
if you wanted to but you made your choice.

You catered to her needs
while I wonder around the city
wishing you were there beside me.
I've known so much of nothing

when it comes to a love that is true.
Everyone around me seems to be
mesmerized by the beauty of the clouds.
And yet, heaven is brighter than the sun.
All the reasons why I wanted to escape
the life placed upon me that hot July day.

Insanity, Pt. 2

Insanity. How can I get blamed
for something I've never done?
Is it because I'm a woman
with the skill to write a poem
with seven verses and sad prose
like the one you hear in sad songs.

Insane and stupid in love.
That's all I'll ever been
when it comes to him.
Call me crazy but his green eyes
was something I loved and admired
but I wasn't someone he wanted.

He wanted a woman to cater
to his own selfish needs.
He wanted to be the first
and the last thing a woman thinks of.
But you, you are different.
You treat me with such dignity and respect.

Insanity. Insanity. Insanity.
Can a woman ever catch a break
from the world she's forced to live with?
Blame her for his mistakes
and his mistakes alone
but never applaud her for the good she's done.

Worse of all, he won't notice
how much hurt she's going through.

He will only notice the things
he wanted to hear from her.
Love him and stop trying.
That's what they tell me.

Are you different enough to change
the way I'm perceived by men?
I'll hand it to you.
You are charming and witty
and nothing like the others.
But are you, are you different?

Let's Pretend It's Christmas

Let's pretend it's Christmas
so the joy of flashing lights
and the star-shaped lanterns
glistening in the sky.

Hanging from the old oak tree,
the wind blows heavy but the strings
is capable of holding onto the stars.
I've made some wrong choices

in my life that I'd rather kept hidden.
Because the world thinks of me
as the wrong kind of girl
who wanted nothing more

than to be loved by someone.
Let's pretend it's Christmas
while we bathe in cliffside pools
and wander around the city

looking for something new to do.
It won't snow in July
but I'm sure August will be brighter
than it should have been.

I wonder where I'll be come December.
Will I find hope in dark places
or will I find shelter in the warmth
of the glowing yellow sun?

I wish pretending was easy
when you've grown since people
dealt an ace out from their sleeves.
Let's pretend it's Christmas.

Joy was easy to come across
when everything is jolly and bright.
Star-shaped lanterns hanging
from the ceiling as carolers sang their song.

Autumn Showers

Fast approaching winter
but I've never liked the weather
when snow hits the ground.
I much prefer the sunshine
and the summer heat
melting everything in its path.

Such sad prose finding its way
in the melody and the harmony
of a song like his and hers.
Autumn showers like spring
gazed upon the winds of the west.
Much more than tomorrow

and yesterday becoming like today.
I've escaped the vast majority
turning into a cyclone of the winds.
I am a wise bird but not like the ones
you read in magazines and newspapers.
I'm more of the girl who had nothing

to lose but herself in the rays
of the sunlight coming from above.
The process of becoming
is like Autumn showers without the rainbow
after we've done things recklessly.
Cheated in games and exams.

It was something we've both done
but it means nothing if we love

the things that come by within the day.
Forty years of your life was spent
waiting on someone like me
to love and to hold in the night.

If I'm Nothing

If I'm nothing, why do you keep
on mentioning my name to your new girl?
You weren't shy when you said
I was the stupid one out of the both of us.
I'm not committed to a crime
we both know you committed.

If I'm no one, then why are you
suffering for nothing our minds did?
You saw me with another man
who is far better than you could be.
You asked him why the girl
with so little to say about her past.

Well, we both know that time
means nothing when it comes
to spending an eternity with someone
worth every hour of our lives.
Still seeing you makes me wonder
if I'm more different than I actually am.

If I'm nothing to you, why are you running?
You said running away with you would be
a treasure and a peace offering of the foul
things I've done to you but I don't remember
ever hurting you the way you said I've done.
You said I'm not the sentimental kind.

But if I'm no one, why do I feel like a somebody
when I write in prose and poetry?

You never dusted off my dusk jacket
and brushed off my sleeves when you read me.
You barely spoke a word to me
at my sixteenth birthday party.

We know there's nothing left
for us but to write our farewells
and seek others with an open mind.
I heard your music from an old friend
she wanted for me to have a little listen
and I admired the words you said in your song.

Dream, Pt. 2

Dreamed of times that made me wonder
where I'd be if I didn't knew you.
I wanted nothing but a love that's eternal.

Began to fade into the crowd
when I'm alone and you've got
your world blending into mine.

I wanted so little to do with the spotlight
but it took me in like it wanted me there.
I wanted to be seen by millions

but not like what you think.
My voice heard by adoring crowds.
I saw you before you sparked.

Little girl and her mother stayed on the bus.
There's no excuse to steal something
that never belonged to anyone.

And yet, we played a fair game.
We became entitled to the things
we wanted as children.

Even at seven, I knew you wanted me.
I knew the things you've felt
when you first saw me there.

And I saw you in my dreams as time passed on.
Seventeen years old, I could be your Priscilla

if you wanted something to hide

from the millions of girls who adores you
because she was the girl at fifteen
who captivated the King of Rock.

Popstar

He was someone known by everybody
and yet, no one knows how much pain
he caused to someone so rare like me.
She wanted to be in love with someone
but he wanted a girl to hide away.

Fate came through for them.
They saw each other in a different light.
He liked what he saw in her
but it's not like what you think.
She was naïve and soft-spoken.

Full of life and a fragile heart.
He took her into his home
and spoke perfect French.
Celebrated every little milestone
with her around as a witness.

He fallen prey and became desperate
to have her in his arms
but she was only seventeen.
What does she knows about love?
Does she even want to be with him?

Questions floods her airy head.
She knows very little about him
and yet, there's only love left
to question in her hour of need.
Seventeen years old in his bed

nothing to lose but her innocence.
Made to act like a plaything
in front of his friends.
She didn't want anything
to do with that kind of crowd.

She was forced to become
someone who she's not.
She wanted only him
and he wanted her.
Wandering eyes got the best of him.

Popstar, I hope you knew
she was someone who you shouldn't
have let your friends play with.
She's burning into ash
whenever she saw you.

Where is your proof that she hurt you?
All she did was love you.
All she did was care about you.
Where were you when she faded away?
Death and destruction was all she knew

when it comes down to you.
Twenty four years old,
you lost her and it got to you.
Selfish boy, nothing good will comes out
of the foolish pride you've shown.

Loved

I loved you once
and when I first
saw you there.
I loved you
in the summer
falling over the city
but nothing as you thought
it would be like.
I loved you
without a single doubt
in my heart
but heartaches like the bitch
you wanted with the world.
People knows who you are
but they know nothing
about me. They know little.

Rainbow After The Rain

Teardrops on the window pane.
You and your guitar singing to me.
I wanted the good in you
to show himself to me.
I gravitated to you like I've always done.
Every moment I've cherished
until you turned sour.
I've never betrayed you
but you fucked up again.
You should know I never
wanted to fight you.
I just wanted to love you.

Don't

Don't spend all your time
on nothing and something.
You'll wonder if it's you
or the view you've seen.
Darling, you're not a magician.
You can't magic away the pain
people feel over the passing time.
But Country Legends are
like OPM singers, they sing with heart
scored by a soulful beat that's honest.
And honesty, can there be too many
words to say how someone feels?
Don't tell me it's over
when it's just begun.
Don't tell me you love me
when fate told you to lie to me.
You'll wonder why I left.
You'll have an empty space
on your bed where I used to lay.

Size

Size. His size.
Everyone belittles him for his size
and they never wondered
why she lost her breath.

Size. His size.
That's just something
that you thought of
when he felt so scared
of losing his good name
to what the men wanted
out of the women.

Change the way you fall over
but there's nothing more to say
when it comes to the freedom
she's got at the party
in his hotel room.

I Said Too Many Words

I said too many words
burned bridges before anyone
can crossover to the other side.
I was young and naïve
at sixteen years of age.
I should've said the things
I've said but no one cares
if you don't have millions
of people flaunting your name.

You've Got It All Backwards

You've got it all backwards.
People don't hurt unless
they have to hurt themselves.
We burn red like ashes
in the midst of the storm.
Nowhere back but the land
that brought us into unity.

Red Wine

Red wine stained her white blouse.
She can't get it off but they ruled her
as an uncultured swine.
She was nothing more than a fling
to him when it comes down to his heart.

Oasis

Wondering where I'd be.
Vanishing from the sight.
I wasted time as it faded.
I wanted to be with
the likes of you
but I've burned through
the oasis of the atmosphere.
I knew the many things
that melted like ice
on a warm summer's day.
I'd still wonder where I'd go.

My Many Phases

My many phases captures
something I don't want to be
seen by others who don't know me.
They see me as someone
who is weaker than her male counterparts.
And still, I write like I've never done before.

Price To Pay

Keep your mouth shut
and your head up high.
That's what they all want
from a woman like me.
They don't see the sacrifices
a woman makes when it comes
down to her being the woman
who has to eat for two
but she doesn't complain.
Once told to abort something
so special before it gains
its beating heart.
That's the price to pay
if she wanted everything
and nothing all at once.

All I Want

All I want is a love
that burns brighter
than the sun most days.
But I'm nothing more
than a wish he never made,
we crossed paths in July.

I never planned on falling
in love with him.
I'm pulled by the world
and I become someone
everyone wanted to keep.
I'm not a doll you can lose.

I'm much more than a witch
who's fellow country girls
burned louder than pieces
of the sky falling down on me.
All I want is nothing short
of complicated.

Love shouldn't be so complicated
when it comes down to writing
a fairytale that two people
can live in when we love and love.
It's not new to fall in love
with the fates and the sky.

It's an ancient tradition
to fall in love with someone.

Blue eyes and charming smile.
The nature of it all
is graced with the etiquette
of dancing in an empty room

with no one else around
but the two of you.
He has never been fearless
before she came around.
That's what they all say
about my mind and my heart.

I Should've Left You

I should've left you
when you tried to take
control of the situation.
We both lost a great deal
of aces in a card game
that was bound to destroy
something powerless.

I wanted all the good
in you as we stroll
down the pavement.
I should've left you
but everything we saw
was nothing more than
a blurry haze to pass by

the shadows of the night.
I ask our friend if it was okay
for me to leave something
behind so I can find my way
back to you again.
Her response was subtle
but sincere. She said,

when all has come out,
one must be ready for whatever
burden the loud will give.
Love at lasts is something
people consider as forever
but is it truly happiness

225

your after in the light of it all.

Stepping Stone

When you went to the Philippines,
was I just another stepping stone?
Was I just someone to defend once?
I love to see you here with me
but things aren't what it seems, you know.
And when it comes to a love that's cruel,
you seem to put all the blame on me.
You had your best days in the sun
while I'm waiting around dying to see you again.
I wanted you to be my full time lover
but we've created a mess out of things.
I never wanted for things to disappear
like it did with Bonnie and Clyde.
I wanted for you to be on my side.
Say goodbye to the girl who I was, darling,
she'll only come back to the one
who wanted her to shine through the rain.
And with him, I won't be just another
stepping stone in a puddle of emotions.

Music Could, Pt. 2

Music could harm us
but it speaks to the soul
when we least expect it.

Music could emotionally
wreck your happiness.
I guess that's the beauty

of an art that's musically
inclined to speak to the soul
of someone brand new.

Music could be something
we put on to feel the love
that we never felt before.

I crave the applause
and the sorrow filled
design of the music I play.

Music could make you feel
like someone new in a world
that's stays the same.

I wanted to be that someone
who shares her heart in music
but things changed with the times.

I changed the things I wanted.
Music could be the devil

we dance with if there's nothing

left to live faithfully for.
Music could be a walk on water.
Miracles and destinies

made to be fulfilled
by the words we seek,
by the words we wanted to hear.

Music could tell us what the boys
want from the romance a woman gives:
torture and insanity, my dear.

That's all they wanted from women.
I guess, my pure white heart
was filled with the fire he didn't want.

That Cold August Night

I wish what you said to him was false.
I didn't want you and the songs
you'll write about me with your band.
But let me remind you that you were the one,
who turned his back from the truth.

I could've been your ride or die.
We could've been like Bonnie and Clyde.
Side by side until there's nowhere left to run.
Said it yourself but I heard the lyrics
your sister wrote and you sang it.

And you are the sad song,
I play when I need to feel something.
You are not Steve McQueen or James Dean
and I'm not your ride or die
when it comes to the things you'll see.

That cold August night I wanted
to see the stars with you
but you only saw her and her lies.
You didn't care to ask me, honey.
Someone else is loving me.

You called me up at 3:30 AM
asking if I would give you the honor
to share the whole night with you.
You told me of what could've been
but I'm happier with him.

It's no good to reminisce about the past.
A Gemini in the sun for four years.
You showed the talent that you've got
to your former friends but it doesn't mean
you were happy to be without someone like me.

But boy, the truth is I still think about you too.
I'm happy and happy doesn't mean
I'll run and run away from the love I've got.
He's my National Anthem and I tend to cry
while listening to Lana Del Rey.

I hope you know it doesn't matter
if we're with someone else.
There's always August and the things
we've done that we haven't apologized for.
That was the best of times, the worst of days.

Oasis, Pt. 2

Sweet oasis in the dark.
Desperate Wives on the TV
and a bowl of oatmeal,
breakfast in bed at 9 PM.

Lover blasting on my cellphone
in my pink shorts and your white t-shirt.
Refrigerator lights lighting up the dark
when it comes to slow dancing with you.

I don't think it's ever enough
to burn with the flames you've lit
when I've bent time to carve my own
path to freedom and independence.

Because in the end, there's shelter
after the rain ahead of us
when we cry to music that freed our soul.
I guess that's the oasis of love.

Just Like Zelda

Get your shit together.
I left you stranded alone
in the arena of war.
It'll never mend my brokenness.

An insane ex-girlfriend
is the only thing I'll ever be
but doesn't mean we burned
our past with the forest fire.

I thought we're lost in the drought.
Fallen over too many things
we've played a part in
but is it just a game to you?

A million love songs
that left us desperate to love again.
What does it do to be over?
We've loved each other

for the millionth time
as the song goes.
But we danced the night away,
and the waltz was all I saved.

I never wanted to be just like Zelda
but you've stolen all the words
I wanted to say to you in the night.
Poetic and dramatic is all I'll ever be.

I guess I'll end up waiting for you
when I go completely insane
from the things I've wanted you to say.
Ancient history is part of the love

we will leave if we break it off
without mending the things to mend.
Love is like a paper cut. It cuts deep.
That much I know.

Warning Sign

I didn't read the things
they wanted me to hear.
I guess the nativity has been
told by the Bible verses.
And here's another tale,
it's not like the ones
you've already heard.
You've been called lucky
when they saw you with me
but the warning signs
was all I've ever known.
Exiled by the times I've spent
on doing nothing with you.
How am I still in love with
the verses in the Bible about
how they dreamed of a better
tomorrow than the ones of
yesterdays spent without you?

I Was Happy

I was someone who was willing
to leave a speck of dust
on the cupboard just so you'll know
that I'll be there to save you again.
I'm better off alone that's what I kept
telling myself when it comes down
to bright lights in the city.
I'm brighter and bigger without you.
I guess it's just another tale
for others to tell to their loved ones.
I was happy to be without you
there to ruin and disappoint me.
Love wasn't something you wanted.
You just wanted the fifteen minutes
that comes with loving me.

Time

Time stood still. It never fails
to disappear into nothing once
we wrote a million love songs
to leave with our legacy.
I've begged all the wrong guys
but you stayed and made things
better than it was before.
Minutes pasted into hours
as time is all we've got
to make things right
but you never wanted
what I wanted.
It's always been about you
and your selfish pride.
I guess all I'll ever be is burned.

Reckless

Start something new
with the one you love.
Different things to share
when it comes down
to all the wrongs we've done.
Ask of me you've made
a careful girl into a reckless one.
Took the letters and burned them
so there's no evidence of the heartbreak
we've both caused each other.
You've fooled me once and I cried.
I wanted you to love me
and be careful with the words
you say to me but you can't
even do that to someone like me.
It was reckless what we had
but it made me stronger
in a world full of desperation.

I Wish You Well

I wish you well. I wish you well.
There's nothing more I could do.
I believed in you when no one else
would. I'm not better off alone.
I just wanted to be loved.
But in return, I've got the love
of millions who only love from afar.

Illicit Light

Ernest Hemingway once said,
"I don't live at all when I'm not with you."
It should be something every man
should say to a fearless woman
just so they could see the smile on her face.
And yet, many men don't recognize
all the sacrifices she's made for him.
He won't see anything else
when it comes to the illicit light
to protect a love affair that's been buried
under passing times and yet,
we've made so many people fall in love
with the words we've shared to one another.

More

The more I start to miss you.
The more I want to paint the skies
after the rainy day passed by me.
I wrote both everything
that passed on while I'm done.
But I'm not lost or missing,
I've found myself one day
leaving the world for something
that made me fall in love
with the likes of you.
The more I love you.
The more I want to tell the world
that I'm grateful to be with
someone like you to hold me.

To Love You

I wanted to love you
but the pain of wanting
was enough for me to suffer.
It was a fragile state
that got my thinking I wasn't
enough for a world full of glamor.
I wanted to have a shot
of happiness when it comes
to my ability to win at something
with a lot of faces in crowds.
I wanted to love you
and to hold you once more.
There are reasons I won't shade
my friends for my own sake
but I've never held myself back.
I wanted you and nothing more.
I know that's the kind of peace
you've been dying to get
from the other girls.

Too Good For A Goodbye

I've said things to people
just to make them leave me
but I don't mean any of it.
I'm too good for a goodbye
but the words seems to come
out just right over my head.

Time, Pt. 2

Time has something to do with us
when it comes to getting to wrap
my arms around your neck but nothing
falls for the Autumn skies.
I'm in love with the beauty
of little raindrops falling
down the window pane.
Don't try so hard when it comes to us.
You are already my everything
that I've always wanted.

Burning Desire

Dry air burned at the stake.
She's speaking in metaphors
but you drowned in the ocean
wanting for something better
to come along, to come by.
Vanity mirror at its bestest
she wondered if she's careless.
She just wanted to be remembered
like Sylvia Plath and Emily Dickinson.
She's listening to Lana Del Rey
to drown everyone's fallen words.
"It's only the beginning,"
that's what she said to him.

Nothing Like Zelda

I'm nothing like Zelda Fitzgerald
but I can paint a beautiful picture
with the words I write on a page.
Drawn like a moth to a flame.
I guess, that's the only metaphor
I know about being drawn
to someone like you.

You are the bright light
I wanted to seek.
You are the poetry
I read it to myself at night.

I'm nothing like the other girls
you've dated in the past.
They wanted attention
I just wanted you.

Sad Songs

If you were wondered,
why I listen to sappy poetry?
There's no reason to wanting
to feel things I'm desperate of.
Sad songs are the mantra
I knew about growing up
outside of bright lights.
But you knew, where I should be.

Echo

Echoes of the wild
burned through the air.
I'm better being the girl
who wrote about things
that happened to her.
You are an echo of the past
that haunts me
until there's nothing left.
But I heard the wind say,
"I love you" so sweetly.

His Girl On A Friday

He has someone to hold
each day of the week.
That's what my friends
told me about him.
I couldn't find it in me
to believe them.
His girl on a Friday
is someone like me.
She's tough but she burned
with the birds on
summer's insane rays.
How could I remind myself
that he would run back to me?
I'm just one of seven girls
he'll play with and toss to the side.

Doodle A Little Number

I've doodled hearts on a page
when I wrote his name down.
I can tell you how he tastes.
But it's sure sweet candy,
how he loves and hold on
to someone like me.

Doodle a little number
without writing down
the things he'll never do.

I could fall right back
into his arms on a Tuesday
if that brings me back closer
to home with him by my side.

Queue The Drums

Queue the drums as we run away
venturing towards the sun
and the faded white clouds.
We listened to Lana Del Rey
and Taylor Swift just so we could
cry about the boys who wronged us.
You told me to take my own advice
and leave while I'm still in the clear
but I couldn't leave a man
who loves me for me.

Young Girl, Pt. 2

Young girl, where could love go?
Have you thought of the film score
that's echoing inside your head?
Young girl, there's still seasons
that'll pass on for you to love again.
He will be right there to be the beauty
you've searched for when you were younger.

Every Little Step We Took

Every little step we took
just so we could find a world
that will welcome a love like ours.
It's a hardship to forget about things.
But at least, we've made our days
in the sun last longer than the music
the band played in the summer.
And yet, all that I've said was a promise
to love you until the end of our time.

Acknowledgements

To my siblings, Janna, Danielle, Francine, and Gavin: You are my rocks. I love y'all so much!!!!!!!

To my mother, Hazel and my step-father, Gil: Thanks for being my first fans and great supporters to the things that I wanted to do in life.

To Trace and the boys of The Filharmonic: You boys are the reason why I started writing poetry. An inspiration to those who came before and after. Y'all made a name for yourselves with the Flashlight cover and I am so proud of you boys. Always slaying every cover and I'm here for it.

To Tom: While you were busy ignoring me, I was busy growing up and learning that I don't need anyone to make myself happy. Because of you, I learned that I make myself happier than ever. You inspired parts of this book. I hope that you get the chance to read it. PS, I will always be the one that you let get away because of your selfish pride and ego. PPS, tell the story of us to your future children but turn it into a fantasy with Princesses and Dragons.

To Dillon: When things get rough, drink lemonade and things will get better soon after. A lot of things have been said about what happened between us. And you've said things behind my back that will only hurt me. I don't like that. I'm the type of person who only wants to spread positivity and kindness in this world. I loved you (now as my brother). But back then, I had a crush on you and I didn't care about gender. I guess this makes me panromantic. Doesn't it?

To Bill and Doreen: Thank you for every advice that you both have given me. I'm a better woman because of it. So, thank you so so much for everything.

To my grandparents, great uncles, and great aunts: Thank you for all the kind words that you all tell me on Facebook.

To my cousins, Erick, Butchie, Bisoy, Earll, Nino, Gaby, Bella, etc.: There's just too many of you to name. OMG! I love you guys so much though. xP

To Jessica, Theyonna, and Caren: Thanks for being my editors and for being patient with me as I edit my work. You two are truly the best. I can't thank you three enough. And thank you for reminding me that my investment in my career is my responsibility.

To my readers: You all remind me that I'm far more capable of loving myself than any man can. And for that, I thank each and everyone of you. I love y'all so much!!!

About The Author

Laika Constantino was born in the Philippines. She was raised in Abergavenny, Wales, United Kingdom. Constantino was enrolled into Art School in 2010 and graduated along with the Class of 2014 with passing grades. She is currently living in Portland, Oregon with her family. She is the author of the Hearts On A Page three-part series and Passport Stamps. She is also a Gaming Video Creator in her spare time.

Instagram: @laikaconspoetry
Twitter and TikTok: @laikacons
Facebook: facebook.com/laikaconsofficial

CPSIA information can be obtained
at www.ICGtesting.com
Printed in the USA
LVHW020600230822
726590LV00004B/168